PROSPERITY AND TORMENT IN FRANCE

CATHOLIC IDEAS FOR A SECULAR WORLD

Jennifer Newsome Martin, series editor

DE NICOLA CENTER
for ETHICS AND CULTURE

Under the sponsorship of the de Nicola Center for Ethics and Culture at the University of Notre Dame, the purpose of this interdisciplinary series is to feature authors from around the world who will expand the influence of Catholic thought on the most important conversations in academia and the public square. The series is "Catholic" in the sense that the books will emphasize and engage the enduring themes of human dignity and flourishing, the common good, truth, beauty, justice, and freedom in ways that reflect and deepen principles affirmed by the Catholic Church for millennia. It is not limited to Catholic authors or even works that explicitly take Catholic principles as a point of departure. Its books are intended to demonstrate the diversity and enhance the relevance of these enduring themes and principles in numerous subjects, ranging from the arts and humanities to the sciences.

PROSPERITY AND TORMENT IN FRANCE

The Paradox of the Democratic Age

***

CHANTAL DELSOL

Translated by ANDREW KELLEY
with a Foreword by DANIEL J. MAHONEY

University of Notre Dame Press
Notre Dame, Indiana

University of Notre Dame Press
Notre Dame, Indiana 46556
undpress.nd.edu

Published in the United States of America

Library of Congress Control Number: 2025934539

ISBN: 978-0-268-20973-5 (Hardback)
ISBN: 978-0-268-20976-6 (WebPDF)
ISBN: 978-0-268-20975-9 (Epub3)

GPSR Compliance Inquiries:
Lightning Source France, 1 Av. Johannes Gutenberg, 78310 Maurepas, France
compliance@lightningsource.fr | Phone: +33 1 30 49 23 42

CONTENTS

vi   Contents

FOREWORD

by Daniel J. Mahoney

Chantal Delsol's eminently wise and provocative reflections on the paradoxes of French politics, culture, and civilization illumine a rich and troubled intellectual tradition for the curious and perplexed Anglophone reader. A distinguished member of the Académie des sciences morales et politiques of the Institut de France, a French political thinker of the first order, Delsol is the author of a slew of books on the tragedies of the European twentieth century (the reader might explore *Icarus Fallen*, a critique [ISI Books, 2003] of the utopianism that disfigured the twentieth century). She is also a sometime novelist, an active Catholic layperson, and an expert on East-Central European political thought, who has earned the right to thoughtfully opine on what she calls the "French Malaise." In this book, she does so magnificently and provocatively.

Delsol is a self-described anguished patriot who is exceedingly sensitive to the deep roots of the French crisis. These are located in the mix of maternalism and paternalism that characterized the French Old Regime, in a revolutionary tradition willing to sacrifice human beings at the altar of an illusory "progress," in a zeal for centralization that eats away at local freedoms, intermediary bodies, and the very notion of "subsidiarity," and in an imprudent desire to jettison the Catholic heritage of France in one fell swoop. Delsol highlights the paradox of a free and wealthy country, with the most generous welfare state and social provisions in the free world, where an insatiable "passion for equality" (as Tocqueville called it) leads to a permanent political malaise and deep-seated psychological discontents. With clarity and eloquence, she shows how modern materialism, hedonism, and individualism have radically undermined the French republican tradition with its emphasis on "communion," national unity, and civic virtue. At the same time, a governing class in Paris shows unconcealed contempt for ordinary people in the periphery. And democracy is identified less and less with the self-government of the French people and more and more with the postnational and postreligious convictions of heavy-handed French and European elites.

As the recent European parliamentary election and French parliamentary elections of June and July 2024 powerfully demonstrate, the French are hopelessly divided between a "progressive" Left that is deeply distrustful of the larger Western tradition, a centrist political bloc headed by President Macron that is technocratic and estranged from France's richest spiritual and cultural traditions, and a "patriotic" Right that is nostalgic for a past that is ill-defined and perhaps long gone. Delsol is a thoughtful and engaged partisan of the Western inheritance. But she stands equidistant from revolutionary impatience and fanaticism, on the one hand, and reactionary nostalgia, on the other.

At the same time, she is no acolyte of the antinomianism and deconstructive zeal of the series of French thinkers associated with "the thought of 1968." She refuses to reject tradition and authority tout court. She is rightly critical of those like Sartre who stated with fanatical self-assurance and an utter lack of decency and moderation that "Marxism is the unsurpassable horizon of our time" and that "every anticommunist is a dog." She is a conservative-minded liberal, a defender of humane self-limitation, a partisan of decentralization, and a liberal-minded, but not radical, Catholic.

Delsol criticizes extreme versions of wokeness and gender theory, while opposing those traditionalists who believe that gender roles are set in stone. Thoughtfully opposing the Jacobin strain in French politics and political thought, she is not a Gaullist since she thinks de Gaulle was too confident that he both embodied and articulated the national interest of France without the genuine mediation of parties and democratic pluralism (not that he was remotely sympathetic to totalitarianism of the Left and Right). She identifies de Gaulle with Charles Maurras, who was a Machiavellian traditionalist rather than a Catholic (and a supporter of Vichy France). (My own view is that de Gaulle was much closer to the Catholic poet and philosopher Charles Péguy, who combined genuine Catholic faith with a patriotism that owed much to both monarchical and republican France.) Like Tocqueville, whom Delsol repeatedly draws from both sympathetically and sensitively (in this case *The Old Regime and the Revolution*), she is not readily classifiable on the political and philosophical spectrum. That makes her thought and prose lively, inviting, and often unpredictable.

On the philosophical plane, Delsol prefers speaking about "the human condition" rather than an absolutely fixed "human nature," even if she detests Promethean impatience and messianic illusions that human beings and society can be transformed at a stroke. Her discussion of the "secular religiosity" of French intellectuals (very far indeed from the prudence of the responsible citizen and statesman) and of the dechristianization of France (a gradual and long-standing process that has gained rapid momentum since the mid-1960s) is both informative and provocative. Yet, she sympathetically discusses the rise of a new generation of young, thoughtful, orthodox, and energetic Catholics in France, a reality that belies the idea that France is simply post-Christian.

At the same time, in her recent international bestseller, *Le fin de la Chrétienté* (The end of Christendom — a book strangely not yet available in English), Delsol argues that political Christianity is finished and that French Catholics must tend to their gardens, patiently rekindling the interior life and the forms of spiritual self-examination that ultimately can give public expression to the Christian faith again. She believes that we live in a new pagan age — pantheistic, this-worldly, and ecological — and that Christianity never in fact succeeded in truly subduing the paganism that preceded it. I do not completely concur with her thesis, but it is suggestive and has given rise to lively and necessary discussions. Once more, as the above discussion indicates, Delsol does not fully belong to any of the parties, whether intellectual, political, or theological. She is that rarity today, a truly independent thinker, one who challenges the dogmatism — and complacency — of dominant and fashionable currents of French and European thought.

This compact book informs, provokes, and gives rise to the kind of deliberation that our civilization very much needs. It is fitting that Chantal Delsol should join Rémi Brague and Pierre Manent as University of Notre Dame Press authors, representing vibrant currents of French and French Catholic thought that are largely ignored by important university presses whose preoccupations are in fact forty or fifty years behind the times. May the reader enjoy this rich, thoughtful, and compact book.

Daniel J. Mahoney

TRANSLATOR'S NOTE

Chantal Delsol's *Prosperity and Torment in France: The Paradox of the Democratic Age* was commissioned by the Institute for Advanced Studies in Culture (IASC) at the University of Virginia. With the translation, my intention has been to remain close to the French text as much as is possible. Thanks to Professors John Owen and Ty Buckman at IASC for asking me to translate this short book, and thanks to Stephen Wrinn, Megan Levine, and their colleagues at the University of Notre Dame Press for their help in preparing the manuscript for publication. Thank you to Robert Banning of Turning Leaves Editorial, whose careful editing has significantly improved the final version.

Introduction

French Malaise

... more capable of heroism than virtue, of genius than
of common sense, ready to conceive vast plans rather
than to complete great tasks; the most brilliant and the most
dangerous nation of Europe, and the one best suited for
becoming by turns an object of admiration, of hatred,
of pity, and of terror, but never of indifference?

— Alexis de Tocqueville,
The Old Regime and the Revolution

My American colleagues sometimes ask me to introduce my
country. A difficult task. For, when it is about that which one
knows better than anything, one will have difficulty setting it at
a distance so as to represent it. And even more complicated still:
it is difficult to describe with objectivity that which one loves.

I am a French woman who is critical of France. One can fondly love one's father or brother and still judge that he is on the wrong path. The same holds for one's homeland, which one can painfully cherish, while helplessly watching its succession of errors.

The number of recent French works that are alarmed at the low spirits of the French people is compelling. As early as 2004, Nicolas Baverez published *La France qui tombe* [The France that is vanishing], and in 2007, Yann Algan and Pierre Cahuc authored *La société de défiance* [The society of defiance], with a subtitle *Comment le modèle français s'autodétruit* [How the French model is self-destructing]. In 2016, Marcel Gauchet published a book of interviews entitled *Comprendre le malheur français* [How to understand the French misfortune]. And there is Jérôme Fourquet, *L'archipel français: Naissance d'une nation multiple et divisée* [The French archipelago: The birth of a multifaceted and divided nation], or Hervé Le Bras's *Se sentir mal dans une France qui va bien: La société paradoxale* [Feeling bad in a France that goes along well: The paradoxical society]. Or, finally, there is Denis Olivennes's *Le délicieux malheur français* [The exquisite French misfortune], Laetitia Strauch-Bonart's *De la France, ce pays que l'on croyait connaître* [About France, this country that we thought we knew], or Pierre Vermeren, *La France qui déclasse* [Declining France]. Such examples could be multiplied: France already has been, for several decades, and probably since the "The Thirty Glorious Years,"[1] a depressed country.

And yet, it is so good to live in France. The citizens are pampered by a welfare state the likes of which exists nowhere else (the number one country in the world for social expenditures; among the highest for gross domestic product per capita, in income growth, in the redistribution of that growth, in the reduction of inequalities, in life expectancy, etc.). Citizens do not pay for either health care or schooling and receive unemployment benefits and a number of other subsidies. They do not worry about either tyranny or war. Not only are the French landscapes forever marvelous, but time-honored and moving monuments are still standing.

And yet "we have the national riches of Germany, the social expenditures of Denmark, and the happiness of . . . Mexico," or, again, "France is a paradise populated by people who believe themselves to be in hell."[2]

Jean Giraudoux recounted a day in December 1909 on which, as a young man, he went to visit Jules Renard, who was already famous: "'I am not busy,' he told me, 'I am unhappy. No. Everyone in my house is doing well. My wife loves me, my children are delightful. My friends are devoted. My play has had success. My books sell. The concierge's dog loves me, too. Family, friendship, and work are all successes. But I am unhappy.'"[3] French people would be well suited to that claim. Fundamentally, in any case, if we compare ourselves to many others, we are very well off. This is why, moreover, so many refugees, passing through no matter how many borders, crash our gates in order to settle here.

It is necessary to try to understand this malaise that is apparently so little justified. For it is this paradox that furnishes the key to the French spirit. France is a country that is simultaneously spoiled by nature and shockingly turned into something ideological by history. The thesis that I will defend in this work is the following: French grief is incomprehensible in the face of the "fortune" and the abundance that can be objectively verified. But this grief comes from a propensity to expect perfection here below—the habit of an ideologue. If one expects perfection, then even "fortune" will seem "unfortunate."

I am conscious of the pessimistic character of my point. The majority of today's commentators are pessimistic about France, as I have noted above. I do not hold that a nation that has been around for more than one thousand years is unable to recover from such a sickness. However, I do not see how it can do this without lucid diagnostics.

1

Identity, History

Nominalism is in fashion, which means I am a globalized individual and without attachments, merely a human being, close to all humans and without relations to any particular group—a citizen of, and in solidarity with, the world, without any preferences or borders.

I believe, on the contrary, that each among us is tied to a homeland, one that he likes with his heart and not just with his mind. The homeland is a particular culture, a history, and a geography—that is, the landscapes, in a word, the atmosphere in which our personal and familial history unfolds. And we humans are made in such a way that the atmosphere of our existence conditions that existence itself. We also know well that what we transmit to subsequent generations has to fall in line with a cultural, even a composite, landscape, unless it is for the purpose of remaining abstract and intangible. The homeland represents the base on which the transfer leans—language, history, traditions. And this base endures a lot longer than any one of us. Here is a paradox: it is the individual man that is dignified, he himself, the one whom we consider as sacred according to our beliefs; but it is the landscape of the individual man that endures more than him and that survives him. This is why during the course of a war such a crisis of conscience can appear: Should we and can we morally sacrifice men so as to save a monument? The ancients, living in holistic societies and used to bestowing more value on the whole than the part, considered that the homeland is an affront hurled at the precariousness of the individual—whence the homeland's grandeur. Cicero writes in the *Republic*:

> Those punishments which even the most stupid can feel—poverty, exile, imprisonment and stripes—private individuals often escape by taking refuge in a swift death. But in the case of a State, death itself is a punishment, though it seems to offer individuals an escape from punishment; for a State ought to be so firmly founded that it will live forever. Hence death is not natural for a State like it is for a human being, for whom death is not only necessary, but frequently even desirable. On the other hand, there is some similarity, if we may compare small things with great, between the overthrow, destruction, and extinction of a State, and the decay and dissolution of the whole universe.[1]

What Cicero calls the state or the homeland does not know a programmed death, as do individuals. It can last as long as successive individuals would like it to and would like to protect it, since it dwells in the atmosphere of their existence. Whence the importance of the homeland, which guarantees by its duration the continuity of the references that it carries and that we, being its children, hold on to.

As will be seen, the current fear and anguish of a large number of French people comes from seeing the values that are specific to "eternal" France collapse and fade away. As Cicero said, each homeland is "eternal." But "for how much more time still?" French people will ask, as they look at their homeland. Today, a reflection on France necessarily is the description of an uneasiness; we will see why.

France occupies a central place in the history of Europe because it was born early and it has known how to play a powerful role during many periods. Its language has been spoken for a long time in many countries. It colonized lands near and far.

Today, one can say that France is in the situation of a formerly powerful and influential country that painfully finds itself given a ranking that is now mediocre and ordinary. For decades, it has succeeded in hiding from itself that it was no longer a star and had fallen to the level of a midtier power. It is necessary to remember the efforts that General de Gaulle made right after World War II to secure a place for France in international bodies,[2] and that in the second half of the twentieth century, his task [*jeu*] was to secure for his homeland the grandeur that, to the extent that it was real in the past centuries, often was nothing more than the hand-waving [*jeu de manches*] of this formidable leader. The Glorious Thirty Years have also certainly contributed to erasing the reality of our diminution as well as the fact that after the war, Germany, bearing the crime of Nazism, hardly had a word to say in the concert of nations. But today, a number of factors, of which I will speak below, manifest and exhibit this diminution that no one can doubt any longer. It is as if a devastating truth, one that had been camouflaged behind bravado for so long, were now to explode in our faces. This new lucidity, with all its consequences, contributes to explaining this French melancholy.

This situation and this consciousness of descent and fall is not specific to France. On the contrary, it is an experience that has been lived and will continue to be lived by a number of home-lands that come and go in history with a privilege and a lot that is uneven over the epochs. Arnold Toynbee, to give but one ex-ample, had even established the distinctive criteria of the decline of civilizations (even if, obviously, one is not able to confuse a homeland with a civilization). Having studied the existing home-lands of Central Europe for a long time, I arrived at the conclu-sion that one of the liveliest of the topics that are characteristic to these countries is what one can call "the Golden Century and the Lost Battle." Indeed, there are people (Romanians, Poles, Hungarians, etc.) who live from the remembrance of their past grandeur, who are constantly nourished by the memory of their former majesty—the Austro-Hungarian empire, or in Poland, the Republic of Two Nations, and the influence over Lithuania. I recall that on the first day of my first trip to Romania, practically before having me sit down, my hosts slid onto the table in front of my own eyes a map of the "Old Kingdom" and of "Greater Romania." This clearly signified, "Today, you will discover a bro-ken and miserable country [this was 1991], but here is what we were, this is our true nature." In order to conceive and under-stand what a heartrending sadness is tied to a fallen homeland, it is necessary to read Cioran,[3] an experience that, moreover, is not always very pleasant because he comes to despise his home-land by dint of lamenting about it.

It is necessary to remember—for the West, in any case—that grandeur does not get good press. Likewise, a French per-son who would glorify the past exploits of Napoleon, who sub-jected the provinces to bloody battles, would instead be laughed at to his face. In our epoch of gentleness and of victimization, one no longer boasts about power, even if it is in the past—and this is certainly not the power that one can indulge in lament-ing. Likewise, the French lament something else: their excep-tional model, at least what they consider as such.

Like an individual, each people has an identity, which signifies that it is unique. Each time, it is an alchemy of multiple
characters that crystallize and together form an absolutely specific "I know not what." A people is always in the process of
transformation, and this is why identity is never set or fixed; it
evolves over time and changes its appearance. A people is
formed of individuals and groups that are transformed and that
are replaced over time throughout history. It loses elements and
acquires others. Yet despite these transformations some specific
characteristics endure and survive in various forms over time.

However, one cannot claim that a people would have a per-
sonality like an individual. A homeland is not a person, regardless of what many authors prior to World War II thought. One
thus spoke readily of the "vocation of France." To speak of the
vocation of a people is a type of shifting of meaning that has
been able to produce deplorable and dangerous nationalisms.
One will recall the doctrine of "manifest destiny" employed in the
United States during the nineteenth century, which conferred
to this nation the vocation of emancipating the world. One can
speak of the "vocation" of a person in the sense of the possession
of specific talents, often concealed, that would confer on the
person preferences and capacities that he or she should employ
for a successful life. But it is in the figurative sense that one speaks
of a homeland as one speaks of a person. Those who do this—for
example, Georges Bernanos, when he speaks of the spiritual vocation of France[4]—presuppose a spiritual vocation that is conferred on human communities and that accordingly is situated
at the heart of a religion or whatever takes the place of it.

Each people finds its own identity in some reality or concept that characterizes it and that is close to its heart. France
identifies with its republican state like Russia identifies with its
empire or the United States identifies with freedom. In France,
the republican state is losing its substance and is beginning to

look like the other neighboring states; the French have the impression that someone is in the process of stealing their very being from them. That is what is going on at this very moment. As soon as one sees a people begin to ask questions about themselves, to ask who they are, then that is the sign of a crisis, of a disequilibrium that indicates metamorphoses that are sometimes painful.

In 496, Clovis was the first barbarian king to be baptized, and for this reason the French were called the "eldest daughter of the church," up until the eighteenth century. In 1841, Father Lacordaire spoke for the first time of France as the "eldest daughter of the church." This primacy, whose advantages the erasure of Christianity has reduced, functions much like the political concepts that Carl Schmitt described: it has not entirely disappeared, but it has been secularized. France, which is no longer concerned about being the eldest daughter of the church, boasts of being the eldest daughter of the revolution. The French Revolution of 1789 elevated the Rights of Man into universal principles, disseminated these new ideas to the entirety of Old Europe, and, thus, contributed to abolishing everywhere the former estates-based society. Without difficulty, France persists with the view that it invented universalism (the United States can say the same!), and, for this reason, it considers itself exceptional.

Exceptionalism is simultaneously a childishness and a narcissism, which amount to the same. But this does not remain a pleasant story: its consequences are harmful. It is necessary to say, from the outset, that no homeland is exceptional.

In describing the characteristics of a people, one quickly falls into stereotypes, into abusive generalizations. When one wants to understand a country, it is, however, interesting to see what psychologists say about nations and especially novelists, who understand the world better than scholars do. The Baltic writer Hermann Keyserling, a cosmopolitan in attitude and a polyglot, had amusingly outlined the character of each European nation.[5] As concerns France, he wrote that "France is a garden and the French are gardeners." He wants to note this mania for cultivating everything, which he calls the passion of form: luxury, flavors, smells, the food, the wine. He adds that this country, the "most spoiled one in Europe,"[6] is the one that will be the worst at resisting great changes, because France, being essentially conservative, will allow what is new only if doing so permits it to remain the same. I would not be able to say this any better. Conservatism is what works best in France. But be careful: I am not talking about political conservatism, the right-wing current that is, on the contrary, utterly disrespected, so much so that it would be impossible for a French party to adopt the name of the "Conservative Party." No, I speak of this love of habit that makes us cherish that which exists more than anything else in the world—the most exemplary item in this matter being the national educational system: every proposal for change regarding this entails, in principle, a revolt. One understands that such a country has trouble adapting to a world that is in a permanent state of metamorphosis and in which it is necessary to put itself in question continually.

If France is doing poorly today, it is, as will be seen, on account of something that has been lost or that one thinks, rightly or wrongly, has been lost, and this is what one could call our historical grandeur. We are hurt by having to learn English while remembering that not many years ago a significant portion of the world spoke our language! We are a country that has been relegated (it is necessary to know families that have been relegated in order to understand what a relegated country is), one that has a tendency to live from its memories, just like an older person who was once famous. One easily conceives how this situation engenders melancholy.

2

Republic vs. Democracy

The republic was born in antiquity—that is, in the age of pre-modern holism. It represents an aspiration for unity during an epoch in which individuals depended closely on one another and that did not really exist in terms of individuals. It is, in this sense, the very image of the political good, if it is true that the good is the expression of the link and the union between humans (the good is the sum-bolos, while evil is dia-bolos, separation). In France, the Revolution of 1789 destroyed the monarchy and called for a republic, having been inspired by Rome. In the eighteenth century, the antiquated, democratic idea had long since fallen into discredit, a synonym for anarchy and disorder and identified with ochlocrats. However, at the same moment, the American Revolution, by putting into place a federal republic, simultaneously called for a republic and the first democracy in the modern sense.

The republic is a political myth.[1] This does not mean that it does not really exist, but rather that it first is a meaningful and structuring story, the history of an assembled people in which social or attitudinal differences are secondary to the common good. The republic had been invented in ancient, holistic societies, and it goes with their communal and consolidated form. In the West in the eighteenth century, the holistic social model faded away so as to allow modern individualism to appear. The revolutions responded to this process: they put into place institutions that are more adapted to new social exigencies. This is the equality of our national slogan. As for fraternity, here you have an advanced variant of solidarity, one expressed within the framework of the nation. It is given as a natural tendency before becoming a morality: one does not force citizens to be in solidarity; one relies on a very human tendency. Man is not only inclined to evil, he is also inclined to good, which means attention to the other. Institutions can develop one penchant or the other. This is what Immanuel Kant had indicated, and Aristotle, well before him: "The disinterested feeling will be satisfied if the use of fruits is made common, conforming to the proverb that between friends everything is in common.... One thus sees that private property is preferable, but that one must make use of it in common."[2] The disinterested feeling is a natural penchant; it is anthropological in the same way as vice. But the desire to share truly becomes tangible for the first time in the family, in which one's brother or sister is in some manner another oneself. Parents provide for each child not on the basis of merit but on the basis of need. As will be seen, the French, Jacobin republican ideal would have it that the welfare state gives to each person what each needs. The enunciation of fraternity signifies that the national society should behave as much as possible as a family. In other words, the national bond would be as strong as that which unifies the members of a family.

It is at the moment in which this bond seems to come undone that one perceives that it is necessary and also perceives the degree to which it is spiritual as much as it is material. Republican fraternity is a sharing in the contrary meanings of the word: one shares the cake of economic growth, and one shares communal beliefs. The shared portion of the cake diminishes, but shared beliefs increase. The two matter, and the one does not replace the other. Using these two elements, fraternity links society into one fabric that is connected in all places. When the bonds unravel, barbarity appears, and this begins with what the Romans, in the first century before Christ, in the period of republican decline, call "neg-ligence" (*negligentia*), the indifference about, and the disappropriation of, bonds. Negligence and the subsequent barbarity are the fraying of the social and cultural text that permits a communal life.

Republican fraternity is a type of civic friendship, of which the ancients spoke when describing a well-ordered city. This is why it crumbles by its very utopianism. Indeed, every friendship concerns specific circles: one cannot be a friend to all of humanity. In all likelihood, the ancients were able to speak of a "civic friendship" only because of the small size of cities, which still were able to appear as large families. The great, current drama of republican fraternity comprises both its utopian character and, in the end, its dissolution. So as not to lose this fraternity, one confuses it with compassion, which has no limit. It thus ceases to be an active and positive principle by becoming a vague lacrimation. The republic suffers from it.

One easily understands that the republican idea is more moral than political. In addition, there exist all sorts of republics that are governed differently (noble ones, oligarchic ones, democratic ones, federalist ones, monarchical ones). Civic friendship is a virtue, one that consists in having the common good come before one's own particular interest. Every morality rests on individual liberty—and if not, it does not exist: only an authoritarian government forces its citizens to favor the common good. The republic thus begins from the presupposition that citizens are freely able to forget themselves in the face of the public entity.

It is still necessary to specify one characteristic of morality in general and, therefore, republican morality in particular, which will allow us to understand the problems of France today. Morality in terms of "you should" is exigent. It calls for effort. It is an action, a practice, that demands a going beyond oneself, even if it is not antinatural. One consents to effort so as to attain a moral goal freely chosen: the republic enters into this schema. It is imperative that the republic has citizens who are fond of the homeland and everything that it represents as a common ideal and who are ready to devote themselves concretely to it at the price of their own well-being. And let me emphasize here: freely—it is not about establishing censors who impose republican virtue; otherwise this will be a false virtue for a subjugated people. Nor is it about decreeing from on high the definition of republican virtue: it is not an issue of science, but of morality, and should thus be decided together. It is necessary to face the facts: the republic is hardly compatible with modern individualism. Can one keep a republic alive in the age of portable electronic devices for music and the like? A portable electronic device allows each person to listen to their own music in public places without bothering others. This is so much the case that subway riders and pedestrians in the streets find themselves isolated in their musical bubble, quite disconnected from what goes on around them.

The republic is a type of community: and the current evolution of Westerners permits them less and less to be integrated into communities. The development of individualism in postmodern societies makes the establishment of a republican community more and more difficult. Contemporary individuals hold on to their differences, and even if they re-create communities around specific cultures or preferences of all sorts, they accept less than ever that all must live in harmony. Made for ancient, holistic societies and revived in the modern era to serve a political ideal, the republican model is probably obsolete. That does not mean that one cannot apply it. It means that in order to apply it, one would need to use force—which no Western government wants to do. In a recent book, the sociologist Jérôme Fourquet described France as an archipelago, which is a grievous condition for a country claiming to be a republic.[3]

France is well known for its individualism, an obligatory product of a strong central state, which spent centuries disempowering intermediate governing bodies. The latest episode is Emmanuel Macron's decision to abolish local taxes, the principal resource of localities—a popular measure that costs the state nothing but that insulted and seriously affected the most necessary intermediate governing bodies. It is French individualism, as will be seen later, that engenders reciprocal defiance.

Today, the contradiction between the republican ideal and the importance of individual wills produces disastrous effects. For the ideal is powerful in minds and in hearts, but it no longer possesses its capacities for fulfillment. No one wants to admit this deficiency. It is thus necessary to put on airs. A process of unfulfillment is at work. The example of the republican school is without a doubt the most revealing and the most dramatic. Everything is said and done as if the public schools were concerned with equality, as if they gave each person an equal chance, even though that has not been happening for a long time. The discourse about public service, about the public function, tells the story of a model country in which everyone works only for the common good. Reality proves to be quite different. Our assets as regards virtue have considerably diminished with the growth of individualism. In the face of such virtue that has become rare, the republican ideal exudes a type of utopia, which is blatantly unrealizable, and is capable only of being spoken but not of being achieved. For, in its proper meaning, the republic is not an unrealizable political form, as is, for example, socialism. It is realizable at the cost of great efforts with a view to the common good. It is not generous ideas that make the republic live, but generous actions, which are otherwise very difficult. Without generous actions, the republic, which of course is not a utopia, turns into one—or, if you prefer, turns into a mystification.

The individualistic thrust in all of the postmodern West—taking into account, of course, differences between countries—announces at which point the republican ideal has and will have difficulty surviving. Is the society inaugurated by Jean Bodin still viable in the era of mobile phones? It would seem not, given the extent to which communal meanings are losing their legitimacy and what little sacrifice we are ready to provide in their defense. French people no longer consider their personal well-being as a territorial ideal—who would fight to save Corsica? But it is more likely that the ideal has changed: humanitarian causes have never brought together as many people of goodwill as they now do, and we see young Parisians driving down to Briançon in carpools arranged with mobile phone apps in order to help migrants on the now famous Col de la Scala. Individualism does not produce a generalized egoism. But ideals change with the times, and all politics must take that into account. On the other hand, politics can provide support for inclinations toward solidarity and encourage the development of it.

The power of the republican idea in France (be the difficulties in its realization what they may) permits us to understand why democracy has had and still has difficulty in becoming established. A republic and a democracy advance, so to speak, in opposite directions. Democracy is an anthropology: it supposes, rightly or wrongly, that all the adults in the city are capable of thinking and expressing the common good. A republic is an ideal of communion, which is quite a different thing. Right from the start, one can guess that the former divides, while the latter unites. Democracy is a political system, the perversion of which is the triumph of the masses, while a republic is a moral atmosphere and hope, the perversion of which is moral hypocrisy. Originally, they were formed against tyranny, but in different ways. One can say that each of them responds to a fundamental human need: in one case, distance, and in the other, sociability. Democracy protects the individual against the bonds that oppress, and the republic builds and protects these bonds. As concerns the former, the goal is the freedom of each person, and as concerns the latter, the goal is concord among all: in a republic, it is the city that is free. One will note that all utopias set the scene for republics (Plato, Thomas More), but never for democracies: this is because the perfection that is envisioned is in the bond—the good entails union, not separation.

Ever since the great revolutions that shook the West at the end of the eighteenth century, one sees America claim a democracy, while France establishes a republic. An idealistic country—some will say unrealistic or ideological—France brings morality to power. This is a myth: the historians Furet and Ozouf describe the republican ideal as a "cultural phantasm" and state that "in certain respects, it is part of the cult of ancients, and it seems only to have been viable in the eras in which humans were giants and demigods."[4]

The fate of holism is not, however, that it is abolished by the birth of modernity. The nostalgia for holism arises in the nineteenth century throughout Europe, and that is not foreign to the republican idea. In individualistic societies, in which the weakest perish without aid, the violent regret of ancient communities produces in Germany a romanticism that carries with it a holism of identity—which later will bring about Nazism—and in France the same regret produces red socialism and republicanism. One knows that the communist revolution narrowly failed to take power in France in 1947. Marxist ideology had been very much alive up until the 1980s. At that time, the republican idea had been swept under the rug: the whole French mindset took up the cause of class struggle and "a brighter tomorrow." But beginning with the moment at which true socialism collapsed on account of the collapsing of its model (the Soviet Union), the Marxist intelligentsia found itself in the position of having to open its eyes. One saw the socialist ideal immediately replaced by the resurgence of the republican ideal. In France, socialism was a substitute for defunct holism (the authors who were most explicit about this were Werner Sombart and Aurel Kolnai), and the revisited republican ideal became a substitute for defunct socialism. Today, it is downright diabolical in France not to call oneself a republican, and, moreover, no one would dare to attempt it. There are republican banquets as well as republican gatherings, the word "republican" qualifying everything that is fashionable and virtuous. As a substitute for socialism, French republicanism has kept socialism's ideology. Blandine Kriegel has indeed shown that the French republican ideal is universalist: it is supposed to work for the entirety of humanity and not for a particular group of people.[5] That is French, and it permits disappointed Marxists to reclaim republicanism as the dream of a dream. In reality, the republic is by definition particular and not universal, since it always concerns a people or a precise community. The idea that one can build a community with all of humanity is ideological. There is no solidarity without a face. It is not on this earth that one can establish the universal communion of the gospel.

Today, the republican ideal, after having replaced the socialist ideal, in turn, withers in disappointment. One realizes, for example, that despite the great protests against communitarian philosophies, the latter develop everywhere, or that school inequality expands in spite of everything. This is why the French are caught in the grip of disappointment and discouragement: when one runs from one utopia to the other, one periodically comes to know moments of great hope and moments of great bitterness. This entirely messianic manner of considering the republic allows us to understand why France is so undemocratic. It has always privileged the union of hearts in comparison with people's freedom. In the twentieth century, in an era of the development of the civic rights of women, France was one of the last countries to establish the right of women to vote (1948): it feared the feminine conservatism that is linked to religiosity. This is a mixture of defiance, which is congenital to all ideologies, and the rejection of religion. I will come back to these two points in later chapters.

However, in the individualistic era, a republic requires a high degree of democracy, because the more the citizens are individualized, the more they must be able to worry about the common good. Changing times make the republican religion less and less acceptable, though its traits remain, having a few perversions and a number of ridiculous features. The centralizing and Jacobinesque aspects, which represent a French way of making the republic concrete, are less and less accepted. In an individualistic society, citizens now find it hard to accept having to ask the government for permission to blow their noses. They now love differences and no longer put up with the standardization that has been a feature of the country since the monarchy. However, uniformization is a guarantee of equality or, in any case, claims to be. And French people are wild about equality. Another contradiction.

3

Jacobinism and Bonapartism

The republic fears democracy because the latter, by conferring power to intermediate governing bodies in the name of freedom, always more or less becomes similar to an oligarchy. This is, thus, how France nurtures a strong penchant for Bonapartism.

For centuries (well before the revolution), France has mistrusted the power of intermediate governing bodies and privileged a direct alliance of the supreme chief (be it the king or the president) with the people. The permanent goal of the French kings had been to diminish the power of feudalities, and in the end, Louis XIV came up with the subterfuge of attracting nobles to Versailles and keeping them there, so that, bedazzled by parties and the revelry of the Court, they would stop thinking about their local powers. This succeeded marvelously, and it aided in bringing about the revolution.

Since the eighteenth century and especially the nineteenth, one can see discussions about this alternative between the power of the lower-level leader and that of the sovereign. In a politically decentralized system, the lower leaders are legion: feudal lords, masters of corporations and of ancient *universitates*, trustees of estates or mayors, and today presidents of cantons and regions, and so on. The authority of lower-level leaders is close to those governed and, thus, linked to leaders' knowledge of the terrain, but this very proximity can lead to arbitrariness (which, for example, one sees in *Les fiancés*, a novel from Alessandro Manzoni, in which an Italian lord in the seventeenth century sets his sights on a young country girl). The authority of a single distant leader can claim anonymity and, thus, a certain objectivity, but his knowledge of realities is less. One can affirm that the choice between these two options, which is always disputable, orients the great currents of politics and of political philosophy. Decentralized or federalist systems prefer lower-level leaders, whereas enlightened despotisms and centralized systems prefer a single and distant leader. This inclination has been clearly defined by authors of the French Enlightenment, of whom almost all speak in favor of a distant leader. One knows of the preference that nurtured Voltaire to be in favor of enlightened despotism, a favor readily demonstrated by his relationships with the prince-autocrats of the day who were admirers of the Enlightenment. In the nineteenth century in France, the same discussion reemerges concerning liberalism: liberalism could be integrated into a centralized or even decentralized political system. There are liberals on both sides, and the arguments are always the same.

Bonaparte and Bonapartism are a very French affair, but they reproduce a type of system that is widespread throughout the old and new worlds. It is a French variant of enlightened despotism, reminiscent of the Enlightenment's infatuation with Frederick II of Prussia, the ideal figure of the learned prince, showing the path of the good to his backward people. Bonaparte fit into the Jacobin movement, which made the revolution into the heir of the centralized policies of the monarchy. It was he who accomplished the work of the revolution and, so to speak, brought it to completion. To this end, he worked to fight against local allegiances and create a new nation—for example, by dividing the country into departments, which consigned the provinces, with their customs and traditions, to the past. "I want the French people to date their happiness from the day the prefects were instituted," he says: happiness would depend on a system! What a utopia! And at the same time, he worked for what is universal: his work is meant to open up a blank slate valid for all peoples. We will find this arrangement in every period: France prefers monism to pluralism because it fears above all diminutive, nepotistic, unjust, irksome authorities—but it especially thinks that the entire earth must adopt monism, and here you have a form of dogmatism. The Code of 1804, which consecrated revolutionary equality, must be applied to conquered countries. Napoleon's discourse is that of a revolution: the abolition of privileges and of hierarchies: equality. Napoleon's work is that of a revolution. And, as one will see later with the Soviet Union, Napoleonic discourse re-creates everywhere other entitlements, other hierarchies, and other fortunes—whether one thinks about the nobility of empire or the prodigious enrichment of the generals of the empire. In other words, under the rhetoric of equality, a *nomenklatura* is already being organized. This is so natural: in the human world, principled egalitarianism would be able to be only a hypocritical posture, one that is immediately contradicted. An armed revolutionary, Napoleon intended to bring his principles to conquered peoples, who sometimes welcomed him with open arms: France abolished the estates, which are hereditary inequalities that were etched in stone and "on the old parapets" of millennial Europe (according to Rimbaud); this is a gift.

Bonapartism is a political monism. In the distant past, France had been a polycentric royalty, in which the centers of decision were plural (in the Middle Ages, this was called the *universitates*: corporations, cities, etc.). But ever since the centralization of the last centuries, political monism has been put into place: out of one single center flow decisions and references, and toward it flow all the results for requesting a judgment. Napoleon writes to Fouché on April 18, 1805: "In France there is no longer but one single party (mine) and I will not tolerate my newspapers saying anything that does not serve my interests."

Bonapartism is a current that is always powerful. It is reborn in each era and especially in times of crisis. The expectation of the providential person characterizes predemocratic peoples. For democracy, and democracy alone, responds to the certainty of uncertainty and comes to be established in societies where it is known that there is no "solution" to a political problem but only trial and error dictated by prudence—a prudence that must always be monitored. A people that loves autocracy will never cease to wait for the good prince, the excellent prince, the perfect prince—which, of course, never happens. This illusion can be found in all enlightened despotisms, or those claiming to be such, whether it concerns Hellenistic monarchies or the Chinese empire. The French are easily convinced of the Platonic ideal that we need a good autocrat, an enlightened autocrat who wants the good, as a result of which everything will be perfect. The political issue here is less about having confidence in freedom than about finding the right governing body. France is closer, philosophically, to enlightened despotism than to democracy. In this respect, there is something immature about France, as can be seen in Tocqueville's painful description of France (given as the epigraph to this book).

Bonapartism is characterized by the obsession with consensus that we always find with a monistic power. Only polycentrism accepts the plurality of opinions, voices, and parties.

It is necessary to remember how much de Gaulle hated political parties and that he only wanted a direct agreement between himself and the people. He protested when his adversaries called him a dictator. ("At this age, would I start a career as a dictator?")

And yet, isn't the beginning of tyranny this rejection of intermediaries? Such is the advice, which became famous in antiquity, that Thrasybulus, the tyrant of Miletus, gave to Periander, who also desired to become a tyrant: "One must cut off the ears of corn that stick out."[1] De Gaulle hated political parties because they represented diverse opinions about the definition of the common good, which he alone wanted to be the one to designate. He was a Maurrassian and in this respect an adversary of democracy,[2] which supposes a kind of relativism and uncertainty as concerns the general interest. De Gaulle also made fun of intellectuals and of opinion makers.

In a completely different register, today we find an analogous attitude with Emmanuel Macron. Since his presidential campaign, he claims to be neither right nor left and finds himself in agreement with all—so much so that commentators make fun of his famous "at the same time." He wants to embrace everything and especially not to have adversaries. This fear of consensus is characteristic of monistic power, or if one prefers, of enlightened despotism. To want to summarize all that is good in a single embrace is to believe that the common good is something scientific, something that does not depend on diverse opinions. This is a rejection of the principle of uncertainty on which democracy is based. Because he won the election, President Macron has a tendency to think that there can be no respectable opinion that is contrary to his own. Whereas de Gaulle's passion for consensus came from Maurrassisme (a current that comes from Plato), Macron's passion for consensus comes from technocracy (a current that equates politics with a science, which is still a form of Platonism). Obviously, these are two different currents, but in the end the result is the same: a democratic denial. As soon as he came to power, Emmanuel Macron hurried to do everything he could to destroy the parties on the right and the left, each of which, to be honest, already had worked hard toward their own disappearance. Satisfied by seeing himself alone as expressing the common good alongside the stunted ghosts of the late right wing and left wing, he then singled out the populist party for vindication as the scourge of the world, against which he is the only remedy (he speaks of "the populist leprosy"). The right-wing extremists of the National Rally are not just adversaries for him, with whom one can discuss issues as part of a normal democratic game. No, they are enemies, which is very different: one must eradicate them, after having called them every degrading name; they must be considered as monsters and nothing less. One must wonder how indeed you can have a democratic power that no longer wants adversaries, but only one enemy: it no longer has very much to do with democracy, which dies if it does not have adversaries.

This tendency of wanting to have a consensus at any price, in order to avoid a democratic face-to-face with different parties understood as adversaries in a fair game, has been visible throughout the Fifth Republic. The commentators are all in agreement in thinking that François Mitterrand consciously elevated the National Front (a party on the extreme right), thanks to the voting method, in order to create an enemy that eclipsed adversaries. It is quite useful to have an enemy: thus, you can proclaim "after me the deluge," and exhort voters to save their own skins (and nothing less) by voting for you. One simply needs to read in the press the apocalyptic descriptions of the eventual arrival of Marine Le Pen to power, between the two rounds of the 2022 presidential election. It is convenient but not democratic. This was a facile tactic for Bonapartists or other autocrats, but a short-term facile tactic ("one shot," the English would say). For the moment, French governors (whether it is Jacques Chirac in the 2022 presidential elections or Emmanuel Macron in the 2019 European elections, up to the most recent presidential elections) are happy to find themselves alone up against a demonized party on the extreme right: they have an easy and triumphant game, they are at war against evil and everyone must lend a hand. But this is a dangerous game because it is hypocritical: one uses democracy so as to play against it. One day or another, it is inevitable that the citizens will realize this and end up voting for the "enemy," when they understand that the latter has been demonized for the sake of the cause. And the "enemy" will have to be treated as such—which means, rejected and fought—the contrary of what it is convenient to do with a democratic adversary. Such a system does not lead to a peaceful alternation, on which a democracy prides itself, but to a war of all against all.

Many other factors demonstrate French people's lack of enthusiasm for democracy. For example, direct universal suffrage is used to elect a president who is given strong powers: this is an exceptional custom in a democratic country, and usually reserved for various autocracies. For this system, which seeks to bring the leader and the people into direct contact, transforms the electoral campaign into a kind of media festival, one hardly conducive to reflection, and gives rise to overt or covert populism. When it comes to large-scale elections, only indirect suffrage allows for democracy, especially when the highest leader has great powers. One could also mention the way of life of the French state, which is entirely worthy of that of the Eastern satraps. All that one has to do is to look at the armada mobilized when the president travels or to experience from the inside the incredible pomp of receptions in the upper echelons of the state in order to be convinced that democracy in France is still very primitive.

It was after *Democracy in America* and after the experience of 1848 that so deeply affected him that Alexis de Tocqueville wrote *The Old Regime and the Revolution*. Whereas *Democracy in America* had been a true revelation about the democratic system, *The Old Regime and the Revolution* is a true revelation about France. The lucidity, the acuteness of the analysis, and the clairvoyance of the author plunge the reader into admiration. Tocqueville was persuaded that the French Revolution, undertaken literally to invent a new social and political world, did not so much

invent as reprise and that it was, no matter what its agents themselves said and thought about it, more of a continuation. But of
what? The continuation of the French spirit, if it is true that
each people has its own spirit, which constitutes, so to speak, its
trademark, its impetus, its specific manner of being in the world.
Thus, Tocqueville throws himself into a study of the France of
the Old Regime. He accomplishes the work of a historian, described in the foreword. He goes over the minutes of state and
provincial assemblies with a fine-toothed comb. He gets his
hands on innumerable documents of the public administration,
which he says provide very precise information on the thoughts,
fears, and hopes of a people. He sees the extent to which this administration holds in its grasp every thread of the lives of the
French people, and the extent to which it has the power to help
and hinder at all levels, and that was so in the centuries that preceded the revolution. He sees the preparation for the revolution
in the image that the Old Regime reflects. How was the monarchy thus able to fall like a ripened fruit? Everything had already
been set into place a long time before. The revolution, whose
spirit would be propagated throughout Europe, bursts onto the
scene first in France because the Old Regime had already erected
the outlines of it.

One always describes the French Revolution as an under-
taking to destroy the estates and their long-standing privileges,
aiming to replace them with a central and centralized government that would implement equality of rights while breaking
down the freedoms of the intermediate governing communities
or even rejecting their existence—which it indeed does. And
the central government would be all the more powerful to the extent that it had broken down more local powers. However, this is
nothing new. How is it that the revolutionary impetus for freedom has, in the end, produced a centralized system and a managed
citizenry? (Antoine de Rivarol said, long before Napoleon ever
lent it an ear: "You will see that this ends in a military tyranny.")

The fact is that the Old Regime had already accomplished the work. Thus, after many centuries of existence, this type of bureaucratic and aggravating government appears to be typically French.

Although during the Renaissance era, the feudal and municipal institutions of the Middle Ages began to fall apart, it was in France that they disappeared the most quickly. And according to a sociological law that Tocqueville would use, the revolt against intermediate governing bodies becomes all that much stronger as the yoke becomes lighter, for the little that remains of servitude seems unbearable. In the eighteenth century, the local governor, to be sure, has his privileges at his disposal (which will be abolished on the night of August 4, 1789), but he no longer governs. And his prerogatives are unacceptable because they no longer imply any common service, but rather only particular advantages. The parishes and promises are already administered by the central authority. The French administrative corps had been massive and powerful for centuries. By means of several dozen high-ranking administrators [*intendants*], it controlled everything — public safety, public works, justice, and aid to the needy. No parish could incur an expense without its assent. One needs to understand that Colbertism — the politics of Louis XIV's finance minister, Colbert, an adherent of the expanded role of the government in economic matters — prefigures and heralds Jacobinism and Physiocratism. In the France of the Old Regime, the government had already become a guardian. Via its representatives, its schools, its publications, and its actions, the government taught its subjects how best to live. The most striking and the most troubling example concerning the Old Regime that Tocqueville mentions is that of civil liberties. During the period that preceded the revolution, the aforementioned liberties were abolished on a regular basis by the king, who not long after resold them to his beneficiaries. This repugnant peddling took place at least seven times in that period, and Tocqueville added: "I cannot find any more shameful aspect of the Old Regime anywhere."[3] And indeed, what does it say about an authority if it sells freedoms to its citizens in order to take them back from them so as to make a new profit from it? The arbitrariness of royal power, which also had the custom of regularly taking away the titles of the nobles and the privileged, only to sell them back to their former beneficiaries,[4] also shaped, in French people, the attitude of dependents and subjects that we find again today. For centuries and even today, a private French company could never be permitted to do what the French state does, for example, when it repays its creditors with massive delays, and, to be honest, only when it feels like doing so. Royal arbitrariness did not die when Louis XVI was put to death.

The disorder and anarchy that reigned at the moment of the revolution were very real. And yet all of that could produce only the opposite: a powerful, central, and administrative state to the nth degree—to which France had already had the proclivity for a long time. In the end, the government took the place of God the Father (which is sometimes expressed here and elsewhere with the term "welfare state [*état-providence*]"). And because that government wants to hold all the conditions of the lives of its subjects in its grasp, as concerns compensation or tranquility (one does not know), it at least gives them the freedom to squabble perpetually about metaphysical questions, which they will not forsake. This, as we shall see, makes the French into inveterate pontificators on all matters that have no reality. When they talk, at least they are not acting. In the centuries leading up to the revolution, local freedoms steadily declined. In the second half of the nineteenth century, this inevitable revolution gave rise to a reactionary political movement that was nostalgic for the old medieval freedoms. The day in 1790 on which the revolution redivided France into departments neither injured nor harmed anyone, because the provinces had felt drained for a long time. This interpretation is essential to understanding the immense credit that French people today give to the state. They resolutely believe that freedom is not guaranteed by allowing opposing powers to develop, but rather via public education, over which the state must take great care. This is a way of looking at things that calls to mind autocracies more than liberal democracies. Incidentally, most of the philosophers and economists of the French revolutionary era were fervent supporters of the enlightened despots of the time. It is not that they disliked freedom; to the contrary: they believed that it was a generous gift from an authority, and not an independent capacity that one would develop opposite it and against it.

But, contrary to its European neighbors, why had France been suckled on centralism and state supervision? How did it become accustomed—and happily, so it seems—to a situation in which no one can set up a charity organization without the endorsement of a controller who oversees every detail of it? How did it happily produce these piles of paperwork that encourage a thriving bureaucracy, the numerous levels of which inevitably give rise to an incredible slowness in decision-making? It is impossible to believe that the French are irreducibly and eternally statist by nature! They are so because of their long history and, historians often think, because of the excessive diversity that forced kings to centralize in order to unite: "We have too often neglected to ask ourselves to what extent, and in what way, Brittany, Alsace, Provence and Paris were part of the same country."[5] Certainly, this is a fact: the attitude of the provinces has been perceived since the revolution as divisive, and in the nineteenth century a great writer like Jules Michelet conceptualized and glorified this idea. To love a province is to reject France. The love of the provinces is understood as one of those old-fashioned things that modernity quite happily knew how to dispose of for us. And the provinces are reduced to their folklore and, thus, lampooned. I will touch on one of the most singular and most lively traits of the French rationalist spirit, according to which to make perfect is necessarily to equalize and to make uniform.

But nothing says that the country with the Académie Française, which is an official agency that controls orthography, would not be able to change its mindset under the pressure of the novelty of time. The country has been molded for two centuries by anti-Jacobin, regionalist, and even federalist currents. The historian Olivier Grenouilleau has recently traced the history of these movements,[6] which are often disputed by a still-dominant Jacobinism, but nonetheless very much alive and well, and often represented by renowned intellectuals (Joseph Proudhon, Maurice Barrès, Charles Maurras, to name but a few). In the second half of the twentieth century, regionalisms spread in sometimes violent or even terroristic ways, while governments sought to rebalance powers from above and powers from below. So are born regionalist reforms, approved by the left as well as the right. The state transfers important expertise to the various regions — whereas in federalized countries, it is the opposite; power comes from the bottom and not from the top: even a regionalized France remains a Jacobin country. Right now, one can feel sorry that the regionalizations have not been able to foment a more decentralized mindset and to contribute toward "curing" the French people of their statism. It is rather the opposite that occurs. Rightly or wrongly, the regions appear to the citizens as fiefs atop which several satraps abuse their opportunities and hire mountains of useless functionaries. It is as if these lower-level leaders were hurrying to do what they saw the higher-level ones do: bureaucratize. The debate continues.

4

A Distant and Maternal Government

This debate has always been present in France: Is it better to obey a single, distant government or a multitude of smaller governments close to oneself? Both, however, can bully you, each in a different way. The first casts over the country a wide, anonymous net that has cracks through which it is easy to fall. The second ones know you and directly watch over you. The French people almost always prefer to obey the higher-level one than the lower-level one: generally speaking, they prefer a single leader in Paris over a number of lower-level leaders in the provinces, anonymous authoritarianism over a named authoritarianism. Voltaire already said this in his own way: "I think, since it is necessary to serve, that it is better to serve under the lion from a good house than under the rats of my colleagues, whose conduct is insolent and ridiculous."[1] This claim, which is full of irony just like its author, conveys a palpable malaise about the subject of democracy. It means that it is shameful to obey one's equals and that in order to agree to obey, one must find a higher-level leader. Democracy is precisely this system by which one agrees, provisionally and within specific limits, to obey one's equals. To prefer "a lion" suggests an obsession with the superior man, an obsession that molds all unhappy democracies.

One will find that in the nineteenth century this tropism is exhibited in the debates about liberalism. The revolution had eradicated intermediate-level governing bodies with the Le Chapelier Law of 1791 and one must not forget that syndicates would be reestablished only in 1884: a century without communities of belonging and solidarity! At that time, it was commonly thought that freedom would continue to grow more and more and that as time passed people would become more autonomous. Here you have the idea of progress that is pushed up until its final entrenchments. Proudhon, in his last writings, claimed that in the end humans will become autonomous and competent to the point of no longer needing a political authority. Only primitive peoples would still require a government. One can say that in the nineteenth century, liberals and Marxists, as different as they were, both believed in the withering away of the state. The discussions about the role of the state are grafted onto this shared certainty. The idea that one has about the role of the state is the consequence of this anthropology and of this historical vision. People have less need for order than in the past, since they are more and more capable of governing themselves. Here the dominant thought is split into two currents. Some call for a decentralization of responsibilities toward intermediate groups (hence federalism and the idea of subsidiarity) and, thus, claim to relegitimize the communities of belonging that had been destroyed by the revolution. For example, in Proudhon's writings: "The directive thoughts are not coming from above but from everywhere; for many things, different groups are capable of governing themselves."[2] The idea of decentralization calls for the existence of groups; one does not decentralize around individuals, without any right to association, a right forbidden throughout the nineteenth century, except for an eclipse in 1848. The second current is that of the classical liberals, who are hostile to groups: for these latter suspend authorities instead of permitting their progressive extinction. Groups re-create hierarchies and the relations of subordination, even despots. For example, Bertauld, a jurist, writes: "Every power, be it local or central, that encroaches on the abilities and the rights of the individual is disastrous for the interests of civilization.... It is necessary, for the benefit of the individual, to arrange guarantees just as much against secondary powers as against higher powers.... As for me, I would prefer a single God hovering above our heads to a crowd of demi-gods whose residences would not be elevated enough for not having a direct and irritating view of my foyer."[3] Beginning with the principle that the reconstitution of intermediate groups would be harmful to the independence of the sovereign individual (they assist and at the same time diminish the individual), liberals will sometimes reluctantly accept a power that is left up to the commune and the association (so as to avoid anarchy and centralism) and sometimes paradoxically recommend centralization; thus a suppression of the intermediate governing groups of the nineteenth century led to centralism on account of a fateful evolution. This evolution is not merely inscribed in the cultural genes of France, a centralized country since the ancient kings. It is also explained in an almost mechanical way. The revolution, which had deprived individuals of their associations and corporations, left them alone in the world and soon obligated them to call for the support of the central state. Using simple logic, we see that an erasure of the social fabric creates statism, since the individual, alone, can do nothing.

If one historically situates France within the politics of Europe, then one finds an original separation between Germany and France, a separation that leads to future developments. Historians suggest that the Gregorian reform of the eleventh century contributed simultaneously to a weakening of the Germanic emperor and to a reinforcement of the French kings[4] — making way for the two political archetypes that would prevail, respectively, in the two places. Since the beginning, Germany always displays and valorizes particular freedoms, while France does the opposite. The Holy Roman Empire represents the beginning of political federalism, at first without knowing it and without conceptualizing it, as always happens. During that same period, France, to the contrary, begins to centralize. It was at the turn from the sixteenth century to the seventeenth that these tendencies were asserted and displayed, via conceptualization, in the antinomy of Bodin and Althusius. It is not a coincidence that the former is French and the latter is German. Bodin opens the path to the concept of sovereignty and confers to his sovereign full power, without which anarchy threatens. He makes way for the legitimacy and the theorization of that which later will be the nation. Althusius composes a theory of federalism — but not of democracy. The difference is that modern democracy will open up the freedom of finalities (citizens decide, for example, if the government will be "socialist" or "liberal"), while federalism opens up the freedom of actions, with the citizens, in Althusius's view, directing their affairs without the government constantly sticking its nose into things; federalism creates free and empowered intermediate governing bodies, but Christianity remains the only possible finality. It is important for my thesis to point out this fundamental difference between the freedom of finalities and the freedom of actions, between democracy and federalism, so as to understand France: for centuries, French people barely enjoyed a true freedom of actions — they have a democracy, but have forgotten everything about the principle of subsidiarity. France is a disciple of Jean Bodin. It would be deemed incongruous to allow the creation of a multitude of minor authorities, connected to the proximity of initiatives and of needs, rather than permitting the stately authority, which is competent and surveilling, to resolve diverse questions and to respond to the lack of discernment and rationality, while the authority of the state is rational, anonymous, neutral, and distant. It is known that corruptions exist on both sides, but in France, the corruptions of the state are clearly preferred to those of local collectivities. In Germany, by tradition, it is the opposite. This is, indeed, why Germany is a romantic nation and France is a rationalist nation. Or, if you prefer, the whole question is that of the precedence of the state or of society. In Germany, society precedes the state: "Man is older than the state," is the repeated motto, while French society is constructed by the state. The difference is discernible everywhere, even if the contemporary period has brought the two visions closer together.

The welfare state [*l'état-providence*] exists everywhere in the West. It is not a French creation, but rather a German or an American one. Today, it is displayed in its extreme form in France and Sweden. Centralization makes citizens unlearn solidarity, since the state now responds to individual needs—centralization increasingly produces the need for the state. The two movements confer with one another: the more the state helps me, the more my initiative diminishes, and the more my initiative diminishes, the more I need the state. When a storm or a flood hits, the citizen becomes indignant that the state did not come sooner. The relationship of the state to the citizen is maternal. Allow us to think about the difference in national configuration between the United States and France. For the United States, the revolution consisted in becoming emancipated from the English *mother*-land and in waiting for the constitution from the founding *fathers*. The French Revolution was organized around the murder of the king, which was symbolic at first, then real, but subsequently it coalesced around the symbol of Marianne, the *mother of the republic*. The Le Chapelier Law which abolished corporations in 1791, forbade the creation of any group of citizens, and henceforth reduced human beings to their individual capabilities: the solitary individual, who is impotent, is going to aspire to the welfare state—and what else can the individual do, without the right to associate when acting? We inherited this history: even if associations and intermediate governing bodies are welcomed today, they are always viewed with mistrust, as we will see later. We have a state that does domestic or economic work (which are analogous, if one looks at the etymology: the eco-nomic is the law of the household) more than political work. It pities us when we are in pain, reassures us, and assures us. And, at the same time, it monitors, controls, and verifies that life-saving precautions are indeed taken everywhere. It is obliged to do this, because if a child drowns, then one will accuse it of not having followed the safety guidelines at the right time and in the right place. It mothers. The citizen begs and is never satisfied: more is always necessary. The state never dares to put forth a reasonable response, by arguing, for example, based on resources that are not infinite. Just the opposite: it begs pardon for not giving enough; it always promises that it will free up other funds. Its maternal attitude corresponds to the infantile attitude of its citizens. The two promote one another.

5

Status and Positions

The French passion for positions of status is as old as the aristocracy—that is to say, as old as France itself. Maybe it comes from the specific way in which the French aristocracy profoundly became a caste, separated from other classes by a barrier of behaviors and proprieties. More than anything, it originates from centralization, which, by making anything that counts come from on high, values only those functions and activities that are stamped and predestined by the state's imprimatur. Well before the revolution, the ambition of every upstanding member of the bourgeoisie in France was not to become a somebody and make a fortune in business, but to be able to buy a "position." For centuries, this ambition has consisted in becoming an immutable actor in one of the spheres of state action. Tocqueville writes that it was necessary at every turn to call for the creation of new positions, remunerated and endowed with privileges, ones that constantly weighed down an administrative apparatus that had become more and more costly, useless, and crushing. In creating so many positions, the Old Regime created a kind of DNA, and we are still here with it. The levels of overpopulated administrations, ones that are quick to create new problems so as to occupy their personnel, represent one of the national characteristics that is fading today only because of a lack of money. It is always jokingly, but lucidly, proclaimed that "the English are rich and the Germans are philologists," which reveals the commercial character of the former and the conceptual of the latter; it could be added that "the French are civil servants."

The purchasing of positions became impossible with the end of the aristocratic society and the development, in the nineteenth century, of democracy. With the nascent democracy, no one had the intention of eliminating these positions, the forever-functionaries who depended on the state, but it was decided to give them to the most deserving. The example of China that the Jesuits brought back at the turn from the eighteenth century to the nineteenth provided a model: the mandarinate. The French system of all-important state examinations, which produces what the sociologist Bourdieu called a "nobility of the state," was inspired by this model. After the Second World War, the Uriage school, a current of thought tied to General de Gaulle, gave rise to the homogenization of the major competitive examinations that had existed for a century, in order to create a single institution for senior civil servants—this would become the National School of Administration (ENA) [École Nationale d'Administration]. Here we have a unique system that exists, to this degree, only in France and China. Xi Jinping passed almost twenty successive state exams to reach the level of supreme leader. In France, one can, indeed, be elected to the high positions without passing a state exam, but this remains rare and difficult.

A young French person can pass the state examination around the age of twenty-two and obtain a certain status and lifelong protection from the vicissitudes of employment and of income.

Philippe d'Iribarne compares this state examination to an early ordeal that defines one's status and rank for life.[1]

The French model has generated a specific type of person, as often happens when the political-social system becomes very predictable.

Having become an agent of the state, especially at the higher levels, the elite republican citizen nurtures a true love for France. And he serves it with all of his heart. He does not want his France to lack even the smallest thing. He has an elevated idea of public service and devotes himself to the general interest with the self-abnegation of a monk. This is why he does not like to have too many personal opinions, and when he has them, he hardly expresses them, and certainly not in writing. If, by exception, he is very unhappy with some action of the government, then he will express this unhappiness under a pseudonym, which is what he calls his duty of confidentiality. Yet, in a general way, he closely follows the prevailing conformism. This "republican" accomplishes his task with a painstaking zeal, and it is probably this meticulousness that characterizes him more than anything else. He considers it petty to be asked to calculate: for France, everything must be perfect. This here is the legacy of the Thirty Glorious Years, a time of greatness (and even, in public services, of waste), and the cost savings that it is necessary to make right now sound to him like a series of embarrassments. Saving money is a game made for the private sector. A functionary of the republic is convinced that the private sector is filled with greedy people who think only about money and acquire it by any means possible, whereas he is a poor and virtuous man who is dedicated only to the common good. He sincerely believes that a state functionary leaves his private interest behind at the front door, whereas the private entrepreneur is radically selfish, even when he gives to charity. If someone sees this republican unsuccessfully waiting for a taxi and asks him if he does not have the Uber app, he responds with a bitter tone: "No, happily I have still managed to

avoid Uber." This signifies that the renunciation of the perni-
cious comforts of the private sector represents a virtue that is
quite difficult to honor. In reality, there is hypocrisy in such a response because the republican functionary is spared unemployment, paid by the state from cradle to grave, and his salary, which
is not at all bad, still comes no matter what happens, even in the
event of absence, of dismissal, of incapacity, and so on—for those
at the highest level, this is a source of income that allows one to
devote oneself to a wide range of other activities, such as politics. However, the evolution of mindsets is moving in the direction that sees the disappearance of this unique type of person. Just
as in the 1970s, when most gifted young people dreamed only of
the ENA and of senior civil service, so since the turn of the century, most gifted young people dream of the private sector. Here is
a change that allows us to understand the hardening of the older
republicans and their bunkerization, of which Jean-Luc Mélenchon's party is a sign (teachers in schools and high schools are
essentially Mélenchon voters, as well as a large percentage of
teachers in higher education).

This method of limiting jobs, or rather of creating titles
with status or positions rather than jobs, has given rise to a phenomenon that is highly accentuated in France: corporatism. No
one can deny that statism and corporatism always go hand in
hand, and this is, to be sure, what has been seen in all the socialist
countries of the twentieth century. Beginning from the moment
at which jobs became almost like annuities, the complete absence
of competition and the complete absence of any type of penalty
gave rise to increased salary demands that become excessive
over time. Public service workers, by dint of grievances and
threats of blockades (especially in sensitive sectors such as trans-
port), end up obtaining perks, bonuses, and privileges of which
no one else can boast. They do not, by the way, settle for this,
but continue to complain, making up a group that, by its very
nature, is outraged and always quick to strike and to protest.

A society where there are only annuities does not work. All the flaws and even the perversions of which humans are capable will creep into any situation that favors them: laziness, negligence, permanent unhappiness. In the end, public services are worn down by the waste and enlargement of more or less justified absences. The French national education system, this great drunken vessel, a system that is simultaneously one of the world's most expensive and most poorly rated, continues to function only because of the dedicated, selfless work of a small number of teachers.

Not a lot of imagination is needed to notice how much such a society resembles that of a "true socialism." Moreover, there is here a genuine affiliation beginning with the centralism of the Old Regime up until our current society of status. For Tocqueville, royal statism is the ancestor of socialism. As concerns property rights that are subject to the vagaries of royal arbitrariness, he writes, "This is the idea of modern socialism. It is interesting to see it first take root in royal despotism."[2] The system of statuses and the development of a functionary class are an expression of true socialism, and to recognize this allows one to understand well the situation. For example, in what manner (a Soviet manner) does such a system use up its capital and impoverish itself to the point of eating its own entrails. It will be remembered that after 1989, one discovered in the cities of East Germany apartment buildings whose floors, starting with the highest ones, had collapsed onto each another during the course of time, due to lack of maintenance, and whose residents in the end were able to live only on the ground floor. The same holds in France for national education or public hospitals: their infrastructures are being maintained despite a lack of money, they are collapsing, and the never-satisfied staff are at wits' end, and it feels as if we are inevitably heading for a debacle. The state keeps dumping in money, and needs continue to grow more and more. This is because nothing was done to take into account fundamental human characteristics: wage earners work better if they are motivated by their autonomy at work and not subjected to the despotic and extravagant whims of an administration, customers waste less if the waste also threatens their own wallet. Instead, France assumes that employees and customers must be given everything without counting on wage earners or customers and assumes a natural willingness on the part of wage earners to work hard for the common good, and on the part of customers to save public money. Socialist thought at the same time erects a society focused on status and a guaranteed economic collapse, due to a lack of taking human reality into account. In a system of this type, wage earners put in for sick leave as often as possible (in any case, they are paid), and patients routinely fail to go to medical appointments (health care is free). Capital becomes depleted, and everything becomes impoverished in all the countries with true socialism, as the history of the twentieth century abundantly shows. France is an extraordinarily wealthy country, not in oil, but as concerns tourism and intellectual capital. It is for this reason alone that it can still be allowed, well after the Thirty Glorious Years, to finance the bankruptcy that a society focused on status represents. But we are coming to the end of the line, even if our governments continue to borrow and spend with little regard to balance sheets.

And so, the following phenomenon occurs: not only does the system become impoverished to the point of ruin merely by the force of its inert, crushing mass, but the more it disqualifies itself, the more it gives rise to corruption, which degrades its reputation and allows the ideology that underpins it to come to light. Let me explain. France is a free country, albeit a highly administered one. Propaganda about public services is powerful here, and the idea is fairly widely shared, at least openly, that French public services are the best in the world, offering free, high-quality services to all. However, this line of argument is increasingly questionable, and ultimately turns into a lie.

The example of education is typical. Even the most fervent republicans realize that private schools offer their children a better chance, both from the intellectual point of view and from the perspective of discipline and order. Of course, there are good public high schools, but you still have to live in the right place, since the "school district map" system prevents one from enrolling one's child in the high school of one's choice. Naturally, the best public high schools are located in the districts in which the most affluent families live. As a result, many people strive to find a private school. Yet it is not so easy to get into such schools: they are limited to 18 percent of all children, by some kind of unwritten law that no one, not even right-wing members of the government, would dare break for fear of "bringing back a school war" (a French fear that resembles great medieval fears). As a result, private schools are bursting at the seams with success, and it is sometimes necessary to wait years before finding a place in one of them — that is, unless one is especially well connected. This is why "noncontract" schools have been created — that is, ones that are entirely open to anyone, although requiring tuition — and why they are enjoying real success despite some major difficulties. One can also cheat and register in a district where there is a good public high school. In short, this is an issue of duplicity and intrigue. What is worse is that only the most informed — in other words, the educated — get away with this, because they know the best way to avoid unruly or censured institutions. We ultimately arrive at a dreadfully hypocritical and perverse situation: most public school teachers are reluctant to have to enroll their own children in public schools. There are several reactions to this. Either they embrace their distrust in the validity of their own school system and send their children to private ones, or they do not accept this paradox, and they resort to all kinds of subterfuge, or they choose to move to a district with the best public schools, or they scheme to enroll their child in programs for rare languages or other specialties, so that the student can benefit from being grouped with better students despite a ban on such practices, or they pay for supplementary education for their child. But it is rare that they agree to see their offspring endure the common lot, which they themselves consider to be very inadequate, even catastrophic. And yet they continue to tout the quality of public schools that they do not want to change even one iota. In egalitarian, and thus unrealistic, systems, the elites — or people on the nomenklatura list — always end up simultaneously lying to themselves and exempting themselves from the common condition. This allows us to understand the ideological character of the French system: public schools are defended by ideology, but it is known that behind the scenes the system does not work — that we allow it to be used by disadvantaged families while we exempt ourselves from it.

The French education system is in bad shape. The generalized body of functionaries facilitates the absences and the irresponsibility of teachers. The ban on assigned tracks for students and the obligation to provide the same program with the same rigor to all woefully neglects the differences between students. This indifference to human reality, which is characteristic of ideologies, can only cause economic mismanagement and the malaise of its users. While the national system of education becomes worn down and pays its teachers starvation wages, the parents of the students, even the most republican of them, think only of abandoning the ship. If by chance a courageous government permits private schools to go beyond the 18 percent threshold, then the private sector will immediately sweep away everything in its path and drain the public school system, killing it in the short term. In other words, we have a very flawed system that remains in place only because of a political and ideological ban on creating another one. History shows that this type of situation does not last.

The case of the national system of education is just one particularly obvious example. In a tradition of public service, which
is displayed and served up with a lot of help from moralizing
rhetoric, everyone is, in the end, searching for only one thing: to
exempt themselves by privilege from common law. For example,
in 1964, amid a general moralistic discourse against capitalized
retirement (immoral because it was capitalistic), a union of civil
servants created *Préfon*, a capitalized retirement scheme reserved for civil servants, to which all contributions are tax-de-
ductible. What is more, whereas private sector pensions take
into account the employee's entire career, the pensions for civil
servants are calculated on the basis of the last six months of the
employee's salary, which is a major advantage. This is exactly
how the people on the nomenklatura list behaved in the socialist countries: either moral posturing or an ideological morality.

Over time, ideological stubbornness produces the opposite
of the desired effect. The egalitarianism of the national system
of education is a glaring example of this. One starts from the
principle that in order to obtain social equality, it is necessary to
establish equality everywhere beginning in childhood. Assigned
tracks and holding students back are forbidden, practically everyone receives a high school degree, and we open the doors of
universities to practically all of those with high school degrees.
Everything is accessible to all, but this is an illusion because differences in ability are already there and they become successively
more apparent as the level increases. It is obviously the less gifted
who suffer from this system of illusions: they leave with under-
valued diplomas that do not allow them to find work. Employ-
ers know all about this and hire based on the level of education:
the children from the upper classes benefit most from these
so-called egalitarian politics.

It is necessary to add that over time, any such system becomes blocked and hardened because each difficulty encourages

it to become enclosed in itself in order to preserve advantages that it has acquired. Thus, today one no longer sees the son of a provincial grocer attend the Polytechnic as frequently was the case thirty or forty years ago. It is possible that the high school in that province would no longer be able to send that gifted young man to the upper echelons. From now on, one passes the major exams because one has received the codes of success: it is henceforth the sons of ENA alumni who are accepted at the ENA and the sons of the Polytechnic alumni who are accepted at the Polytechnic. The data on this subject are persuasive and terrifying. The story of Albert Camus, an orphan — raised by an illiterate mother — who attended state schools but went on to win the Nobel Prize for literature, is a story that is no longer possible today, because one can see how the system of status allows a track in school to become a caste. In another realm, it is much easier for the son of a railway worker to become a railway worker — statuses are passed on by family because they have become rarer and because a narrowing of the system, over time, was inevitable.

It is obvious today, and it has been so since the turn of the century, that the system of status is on trial and that all is being done so as not to put a stop to it (it is only in Switzerland where one can remove the status of functionaries by decision), but to chip away at it as much as possible. This is very difficult to achieve because by definition a corporation holds on to its privileges and is ready to use any means necessary, no matter how low (for example, to hold up all the trains in a country for weeks), in order to preserve them. Today, it is becoming rarer that public service hires functionaries: instead, it increasingly employs contract workers, which obviously makes corporations cringe and elevates Jean-Luc Mélenchon's party. This questioning of the system of status is the result of a lucidity about the ideological character of this system. But even if a large number of elected officials were to understand the utopianism of it, the majority of them would not have the courage to stand up to these corporations, from which they only receive blows. The questioning is solely the result of the issue of costs: to keep things going, it would be necessary simply to have the Danaids' barrel. In other words, the system comes to be questioned only on the basis of economic distress, which happened to countries with true socialism.

But what is most important with this affair lies elsewhere: the crux of the questioning of the system of status rests in French neurasthenia. It is quite necessary to see that French public service, which employs one-third of the population and which sustains a large number of sectors, had been considered in France as the "French social model" par excellence. During the half-century after the Second World War, not a day passed in which one of our government officials did not counsel a foreign country to imitate this model as a paragon of social justice and of success, from all points of view. There were decades in which it was impossible to do any bench-marking because one does not compare the French model, which, by definition, is incomparable. This affection, which is shared by a large part of the population, was without a doubt ideological, but, in any case, it conveyed a love of the homeland and, as such, merits respect. It is related to French universalism, about which Keyserling wrote: "The French person is altogether incapable of understanding why any one wants to be different from him; and if an individual just cannot resemble him, he regards this as something temporary, and offers his assistance generously and in all disinterestedness."[3] There are homelands that are carried away by a tenacious inferiority complex (Romania, for example, as one sees in Cioran's writings or today in Cărtărescu, or in Ukraine as one sees in Zabouzhko's works). France is afflicted with a tenacious superiority complex—which is not any more glorious.

This intolerant vision of universalism is in the process of becoming undone in France and elsewhere. And this erasure is involved in the anxiety of the French: a people that has the habit of believing itself to be a model finds itself disoriented when it loses this interior compass.

In the end, simply claiming that this model does not work, that it is lagging behind developed countries, that common sense claims to transform it, gives rise to a desperation whose magnitude is hard to conceive. Simply thinking that we must resign ourselves to a more liberal economic and social model, one that is more given over to competition, taking into consideration both the fear of being fired and a desire for profit, is a horrible deception. For our system was supposed to be based solely on dedication to public service—it has been known that this is not really the case, but that we pretended to ignore it. At bottom, what is happening to us right now is a great disappointment vis-à-vis the necessity of facing up to and dismissing a utopia that has been camouflaged up to this point. Philippe d'Iribarne has shown the surprising resistance of this archaism and the extraordinary affection of the French people for an outdated model that always and everywhere has demonstrated its incompetence.[4]

The consequence of this enormous deception is a profound and gloomy socioeconomic conservatism: the slogan of the French people is "it was better before." The country lives off of the nostalgia for an era in which our "model" worked. It has the feeling that it is sinking ever deeper into the doldrums, and this is why it refuses any new reforms. As Marchel Gauchet said, "One can imagine the alternative only in terms of a regression."[5]

Today, the system of merit regarding positions (via major state examinations) and the prevailing corporatism have been widely criticized by a portion of French public opinion. This happens to such an extent that the coming dissolution of the ENA is periodically announced—so, at least the issue is being raised. And President Macron has searched for any means to weaken the privileges of the corporations: this is a first because no president before him had dared to attack these bastions. He challenges head-on the status of railway workers or the pensions of functionaries, which are generous with respect to all the others. It is not a certainty that he will manage to put an end to these privileges that have all the telltale signs of the Old Regime. For those who make use of them have an extremely pointed response. One can wonder about the arguments with which these privileged people justify their exceptional benefits. Curiously, they have neither shame nor difficulty in doing this: they argue that this is fair compensation for a lower salary (which has been false for years now and in many sectors); they argue based on history and on past contracts; they argue based on their mission of public service, which is worth its weight in gold. In a nutshell, they defend their exceptionality based on the fact that they serve the state. It is easy to see today that this line of defense becomes less and less credible, and this decrease in credibility occurs less for reasons pertaining to virtue (privileges are always undeserved in a democracy) than for economic reasons. When unemployment is high and when poverty spreads through the population, this group of lifelong employees endowed with such benefits literally becomes incongruous. And as this group represents approximately one-fourth of the population (but that depends on how one calculates this, as there are intermediate statuses, too), the situation engenders within this important group a bitterness, a revolt, a feeling of being at the end of the world, which gives rise to and amplifies French neurasthenia. However, one cannot see how France would be able to preserve a system as archaic as this one in an open and impoverished world. The upper ranks of the civil service, in particular, seem to be a privileged caste, and a very costly one at a time when the Thirty Glorious Years are well behind us. I share Marcel Gauchet's opinion when he calls for "a night like August 4th for the French nomenklatura."[6]

6

The Anthropology of Defiance

Envy, Equality, and Mistrust

The longevity and the permanence of Colbertism in economics and of Jacobinism in politics have produced the characteristics of France that we see right in front of our eyes. How true it is that when one lives a long time with a certain order that is considered to be legitimate, it orients one's temperament. It is necessary to add, and fortunately so, that the collective characteristics that can be recognized in a people are not definitive. In this regard, it is not a matter of an essence, but of a way of being and thinking that is linked to customs and laws. Such a way of being and thinking can be transformed according to the mixtures of culture (immigration), external events (globalization), and currents of thought and methods of government (the recent replacement of socialism by liberalism). However, it is necessary to express these characteristics, albeit cautiously, if one wants to attempt to understand a country.

What are the anthropological presuppositions that underpin the social-political-economical organization that I have just described?

In the first place, the successive political organizations since the absolute monarchy posit the hypothesis, or the certainty, that subjects are incapable of managing their affairs without the help of a public authority. Every autocracy considers, to varying degrees according to eras and places, that the subject is immature. It frequently happens that autocrats make themselves out to be "the father of the people" (in China, "the father and mother of the people"), confirming the definitively childish nature of lambda individuals, who cannot decide their complete destiny on their own. This way of seeing things is decisive and displays the origin of the policies in question. The other way of seeing things—for example, that of Althusius or federalism in general—conversely assumes that the individual is an adult, capable alone of governing himself and deciding his own destiny. French people are amazed when they realize that health care in the United States is not a right guaranteed by the state, but depends on uncertain private insurance. They believe that citizens are generally not capable of running this risk alone and that at a minimum it should be obligatory to have health insurance. And so it was that at the turn of the century, France was second only to Belgium as the Western country with the most formalities involved in setting up a business.

All of this, as one can see, is a question of anthropological belief. Neither of the two points of view is rational. There are arguments in both directions. The French point of view is deeply rooted in specific attitudes. In 2019, certain administrative authorities realized that several villages in the Hautes-Alpes region had themselves been directly managing (for centuries) the canal system that irrigates their land, based on local cooperative oversight. The energy, the vehemence, and the level of enforcement measures with which the administration set about taking over this collective work from the unfortunate villagers gave lip service to sympathy but made grand declarations about competence reminiscent of ones that always come from on high. Clearly: the water (which comes down from the glaciers) is too serious a matter to be entrusted to the citizens—a functionary is necessary for that.

As soon as matters move past the individual level and into the public domain, even if the magnitude is small, one finds oneself before a new certainty: private citizens are never capable of dealing with the public good; by definition they are concerned only with their own particular interests. This is no longer a question of inability or immaturity, but of an impossibility of getting outside of oneself—in short, of a lack of generosity.

Commentators are in agreement in stating that individualism is one of the characteristics of the French people and that Colbertism and Jacobinism have inevitably produced forms of individualism. Tocqueville described how the erasure of intermediate governing bodies and their powers produces a disjointed society.[1] For intermediary governing bodies develop solidarity and weave social relations, whatever may, otherwise, be their possible corruptions. Without them, that which has complete power and the disempowered citizen find themselves face-to-face. Each disarmed citizen thinks only, to the detriment of others, of saving his or her own skin. The French tropism toward forms of despotism, together with monarchical absolutism, has given rise to one of the most individualistic nations in Europe. Tocqueville describes it in this way: "The government of the Old Regime had already taken away from the French any possibility or desire of helping one another. When the Revolution happened, one would have searched most of France in vain for ten men who had the habit of acting in common in an orderly way."[2]

Philippe d'Iribarne, in his celebrated book *La logique de l'honneur* [The logic of honor], has shown how the relationships of authority within businesses differ enormously from one country or a group of countries to another.[3] In the Anglo-Saxon world, the logic of the contract predominates. A contract presupposes a type of equality between the parties involved and a level of confidence, as well as the expectation of receiving a fair return for what one gives. The logic is wholly different in France: with relationships of authority, what is essential is not to lose face, to receive the consideration that is due to you. It is necessary to remain dignified and to shine, even if the situation demands obedience. This overvaluing of personal honor is the legacy of the monarchical and aristocratic world. In *The Spirit of the Laws*, Montesquieu said that the spring of a monarchical government (not to be confused with despotism, which governs arbitrarily, whereas the monarch establishes laws) is honor.[4] Honor presupposes that everyone loves and demands distinctions and ranks — that is, exceptions, if you will. It presupposes that all love themselves very much and deem themselves to be rare and precious in their singularity. Montesquieu wrote: "The nature of honor is to demand preferences and distinctions."[5] This is very clear to the French people. They love their status for the special benefits they draw from it, benefits that reflect a person's importance and worth. If someone talks of reducing the benefits linked to their status (especially long vacations, extra carefully designed pension plans, special bonuses, etc.), they become indignant and revolt, as if someone were treating them like slaves. It is important to understand that it is not just about the material or financial nature of these distinctions: it is also about their symbolic nature — they attest to the grandeur of the individual who has earned them. They represent the person's honor.

Hervé Le Bras writes about "egalitarian individualism, the heart of national culture."[6] Indeed, a complicated dialectic is established between individualism and one's sense of honor, egalitarianism, and the culture of envy.

France is, along with Sweden, the most egalitarian country in Europe—that is, in the West—and in the world. But each of these countries gets its character on account of a different history.

Before the revolution, France had become used to exempting rich people from taxes and of making poor people pay them. It would not be necessary to believe that this mind-boggling method, which was described ironically by Louis de Funès in one of his films, was routine in the country of the Old Regime. This was not the case with the English. In France, it undoubtedly produced a hatred of the rich that was to carry deleterious fruits into the future. Class differences were extraordinarily marked in France under the Old Regime, to the point where—or so said the philosophers—the nobles assumed that their servants were not truly human. It is likely that the humiliation resulting from this state of affairs produced, just as it did later in Russia, a most bloody revolution. Human beings are profoundly equal at their core: both in the tragedy of their fate and their quest for meaning in life. To separate them radically by titles and ways of being comes off as a gratuitous humiliation. I believe that the Third Estate in France has never forgiven this. It has made us pay for this forever and ever. It would be difficult to find a nation where the rich are so loathed (François Hollande, then first secretary of the Socialist Party, declared in 2006 on France 2: "Yes, I do not like rich people, I do not like the rich, that is agreed").

French persons clearly prefer equality to liberty: they prefer everyone to be dealt with in the same manner, even if it means losing some of their freedom instead of suffering the inequalities to which freedom gives rise. In other words, their sense of equality extends to egalitarianism. This can lead to an understanding of fraternity as the erasure of differences. This is what happens when every difference is called "discrimination" or when individual merit, an essential quality of liberal society, is criticized in the same way as any inequality of wealth or birth.

It is on the criticism of individual merit that socialist society is based: we cannot even stand the fact that some people are more talented or more courageous than others. So everything has to pass by a measuring stick. A school policy, such as the abolition of evening homework, is typical in this respect: it is necessary to prevent some students from giving themselves more time to work or to prevent some parents from taking the trouble to make their children work. The French left feels that, in today's liberal society, which is henceforth ours, individual merit has replaced the former criteria relating to hierarchy. And they regret that a hierarchy still exists. To explain this, Denis Olivennes published a famous text twenty-five years ago in the *Cahiers de la Fondation Saint Simon* entitled "La préférence française pour le chômage" (The French preference for unemployment). He showed that in France, equality among people who receive unemployment benefits is preferred over risking inequality among workers based on merit; having a society with many unemployed people is preferred over having many people employed in "little jobs." Recently, in 2020, the same author reiterated these points by writing, "Here, unemployment is not a problem, it is a solution."[7]

One of my friends laughs when he says that the French left "never got over not having paved the way for communism in 1947" (it must be remembered that at that time the Communist Party had almost taken over power in the country): when it comes to decrying the inequality of merit, there is no other solution than communism—destroying families and sending intellectuals to work in the fields. This is, indeed, the despair of the French left: always cherishing the egalitarian ideal that can be attained only via terror.

The egalitarian spirit leads to individualism and materialism. For it promotes, above all, what is specific to equality and what can be shared: money. It also favors fratricidal struggles, since the only thing possessing value (matter) is restrictive: it is a cake, which can be cut into pieces, whereas immaterial goods, on the contrary, unfold by being shared. Since the only good that is valued is material well-being and consumption, one rebels in order to receive an equal share of consumption. One would not revolt over spiritual goods: they cannot be accounted for or equalized; they are not distributed from outside, but are internal in terms of access and evaluation. The egalitarian spirit gives rise to materialism, and materialism develops egalitarian uprisings.

Hatred of the wealthy gives rise to an appeal to the state. In France, we do not like patronage, which we tend to see, in the words of Moses I. Finley, as "a ritualization of inequality." State subsidies are much preferred over individual generosity. Subsidies are anonymous (of course, they are provided by taxes, but anonymously), whereas individual generosity is flaunted and boasted, and, thus, it humiliates. After the fire at the Notre Dame Cathedral in Paris in April 2019, many French industrialists announced enormous gifts. A controversy immediately ensued: this money was not wanted; what would have been better is that the needed money come from the state; a tax deduction is not required, and so on. Indignation grew due to this surge of hundreds of millions of Euros, made possible by tax deductions. One could call this generosity hypocritical because it is too easy. To mitigate the controversy, the Pinault family announced its decision to forgo any tax deduction on its donations. In other words, even in the face of an event as serious as the fire at Notre Dame and the financial requirements tied to its reconstruction, in the weeks after the fire, French public opinion was concerned only with one thing: preventing patrons of the arts from gaining notoriety from their gesture, disparaging their generosity, and making them appear like vultures chasing after glory.

The republican ideal in France is understood more as egalitarian than as a union that would respect diversity. There is distrust with regard to concerns about diversity as they contain hidden hierarchies. The country would be able to be republican only if the state were to decide for everyone about minimum wages, working hours, school curricula, retirement age, and so on. French people tend to think that only equality, in the sense of measuring up to some standard, can allow for citizens to come together or can give rise to a kind of union of the hearts.

Perhaps all of this allows us to understand the paradox mentioned by the sociologist Hervé Le Bras: in France, even though social redistribution is one of the best in the world, French people feel unprotected and ceaselessly criticize the welfare state for its shortcomings. The title of his book is *Se sentir mal dans une France qui va bien: La société paradoxale* [Feeling bad in a France that goes along well: The paradoxical society]. This declaration, made during the time of the "Yellow Vests" ["Gilets Jaunes"] crisis, suggests that the greater is the equality, the greater is the feeling of inequality, at least when we come out of an ideological period fed by egalitarian utopias (a very large number of French people are former Marxists). So, the media are replete with indignation in the face of the inequalities that become more diverse: children who go to school without having had breakfast suffer from inequality (some think that the state should offer breakfast to everyone, and in fact elected representatives made proposals along these lines at the time of the Yellow Vests crisis); it is unbearable to watch student rents increase: it is an inequality vis-à-vis education (remember that in France, a university education is public and free); or even that the five fruits and vegetables needed daily for good health are not equally accessible to all—this is unacceptable.

One is going to think immediately: But how can this egalitarianism come to terms with the thirst for privilege that I mentioned earlier? Here you have the crux of French singularity. The love of privileges comes from a monarchical and aristocratic era. Egalitarianism comes from the socialism that is deeply rooted in France. The two together presuppose individualism and a certain vision of freedom. While for an Englishman, freedom is linked to private property and for a German to his place in the community, for a Frenchman, freedom is linked to the person who, on account of superior rank, is not forced to submit to another.[8] Freedom is linked to individual honor. It is also necessary to say that these two characteristics, egalitarianism and the love of privileges, constantly clash in real life, producing the permanent fact that the privileges of status must remain hidden: one does not speak of them, one deceitfully denies them, and one finds ways to hide them. This just goes to show the extent to which they contradict the reigning egalitarianism. Hence, there is mistrust, another characteristic of the French mentality.

Denis Olivennes has clearly shown, as concerns France, that the statist-corporatist system gives rise to division and mistrust.[9] When one loves France, as I do, one cannot read a more distressing book than the one by Algan and Cahuc.[10] All the country's towering weaknesses and vices appear, classified and counted, in broad daylight. This is a life-size measure of profound depression, melancholy, and dark pessimism; and all of that against a backdrop of economic wealth, technical success, real democratic freedom, and extreme, egalitarian redistribution on all fronts.

Is this a paradox or the consequence of a historic manner of living? Before discussing the causes, allow me quickly to describe the facts, as obtained from the data in sociological surveys. Among the twenty-seven European countries, France is always in the top three or four on the ladder as regards phrases with positive answers to questions such as "To get to the top, you need to be corrupt," or "I have no confidence in the system of justice," or "I have no confidence in Parliament," or "I have no confidence in the trade unions," or "one cannot trust others." As one might expect, this distrust of others corresponds to personal incivility: I assume that others will behave as I do. Thus, of the twenty or so of the world's largest countries questioned in the World Values Survey, France is last or second-to-last for negative responses to the following questions: "Is it ever justifiable unduly to receive public aid?," or "Is it ever justifiable to buy something that one knows is stolen?," or "Is it ever justifiable to accept a bribe while performing one's duties?"

French society is a society in which mistrust erupts with every step. Many French people have no confidence in institutions, the justice system, trade unions, the private sector, or Parliament, and they believe that all rich people are corrupt, and so forth. Charles de Gaulle wrote in his *Mémoires d'espoir* [Memoirs of hope]: "Social relations remain marked by mistrust and bitterness. Each person has a feeling for what he lacks rather than what he has."[11] This tropism presumes envy, aggression, class warfare, and mutual surveillance. Commentators believe that there has been a deterioration, in this regard, since the Second World War: Algan and Cahuc speak of the "Vichy syndrome," which is said to have given rise to a historic pessimism among the French. The studies that are available to us make note of this trend beginning with the middle of the twentieth century. However, the causes of this mindset are probably more profound (for example, we do not witness the same pessimism in Germans, who suffered the full force of the historical collapse). For Algan and Cahuc, the French mix of corporatism and statism produces this result. Statism dries up competition and favors corruption. Corporatism, which develops special, hidden statuses, encourages envy and suspicion. The ordinary citizen knows, for example, that the railway worker benefits from bonuses and the teachers benefit from long vacations, but he does not know the extent of these, because the two corporations never talk about them or make their numbers public. In society, every opacity gives rise to distrust, yet French society is completely opaque in this respect. G. Esping-Andersen classifies France as a conservative, corporatist welfare state: the main purpose of state spending is to preserve status.[12]

7

Paris and the Provinces

Under the absolute monarchy of Louis XIV, the French nobility settled in at Versailles in order to parade around at the court of the king. So they deserted the provinces and ceased to be concerned about them. This move was desired by the king, who anticipated watching over the aristocracy and diverting them from their reprehensible desires in order to diminish local rights. All autocracies in history have sought to exhaust or defeat aristocracies, which are their most acute threat. The aristocracy's move to Paris estranged them from the people, whom they no longer knew, and that gave rise to specific social breakdowns that we find again today: the Parisian person and the provincial one are separated not only by geography but also by culture.

The extreme dominance of the capital over the provinces is a French evil that every writer knows and deplores. Consider Tocqueville, who quotes Montesquieu: "As early as 1740, Montesquieu wrote to one of his friends: *In France, nothing exists but*

Paris and the distant provinces, because Paris has not yet had time to devour them."[1]

The peril that lies waiting for every society is its dissociation: civil peace comes from a certain bond, transcending particular interests, that unites citizens. This can be, as in the United States, the love of country or perhaps a common religion. The French call this bond "fraternity" and cite it in their national motto. The loss of this bond is a great danger, as Cicero said of republican Rome, in regard to Scipio's dream: "Scipio tries to find out why it is that two suns have been seen, instead of trying to find out why there are two senates and almost two peoples in one and the same Republic."[2] It is one of the threats that lie waiting for Western countries today, and this brings about the phenomenon known as populism. Above all, France finds itself threatened by this phenomenon because of the permanent dissociation between its capital and its provinces that it has kept up for centuries. The phenomenon known as "Paris" represents a perpetual source of internal dissociation, and quite naturally it plays a key role in the crisis of democracy as viewed from the French perspective.

The phenomenon of geographical centralization is typically French, even if other countries, such as England, are also prone to it in some way. In France this has been long-standing, dating back to the monarchy, and is, thus, deeply embedded in the French mindset. In *The Old Regime and the Revolution*, Tocqueville writes concerning old France: "But its only source was Paris." "The movement of thought no longer originated anywhere but at the center. Paris had succeeded in devouring the provinces."[3] Already under the monarchy, "Paris had become the master of the nation, when up to then it had merely been its capital, or rather had become the entire country itself."[4] And Tocqueville writes, when recounting Arthur Young's famous trip to French provinces at the time of the revolution: "Young asked the inhabitants what they were going to do. The response is the same everywhere, he says. We're only a provincial town, we'll have to see what they'll do in Paris. . . . These people do not even dare to have an opinion, he adds, until they know what they think in Paris."[5] Tocqueville wanted to show that French geographical centralization did not begin with the revolution, but rather went much further back in history. It is likely the fruit of an authoritarian type of monarchy. And in this respect, eras are similar because they all originate from the same matrix. The last kings lured the nobility to Versailles and had them mingle about at court so that they would not want to plot against the kings. In the end, the nobility lived in a world completely removed from that of the people in the provinces. The same holds true today for the elite, cosmopolitan Parisian, who, in the words of Thomas Frank, lives like a tourist in his own country.

It is necessary to say a few words about this question of the capital and the provinces if we are to tell the story of France. It is an essential part of our history, and it has become an element of our disposition. Many French authors have described it. I would like to mention two of them in particular: Honoré de Balzac and François Mauriac. Both were fascinated by this phenomenon.

Balzac and Mauriac, with almost a century between them, shared, in this respect, the fate of most French writers, thinkers, and rulers: they were born in the provinces and then moved to Paris when the time came for them to think, write, and act. We say "ascended" to Paris. This could mean a journey from the south to north, since the capital is located in the north of the country. But above all, it is a question of hierarchy: one "ascends" to a higher spot. Balzac invented the character of Eugène de Rastignac, whom he portrayed in several of his novels: the small provincial man who "ascends" to Paris to acquire fame and fortune. This character became the symbol of a very French phenomenon: "a Rastignac" means a schemer consumed with ambition and who is ready to do anything to be elevated.

In France, the difference between Paris and the rest of the country is such that the rest of the country seems to be undifferentiated: a Parisian will say that he is leaving for "the provinces," which means anywhere outside of Paris. By the way, one need only look at the railroad map: everything converges on Paris, and to go from one part of the country to another, one often needs to travel via Paris, at the cost of a greater distance.

The antithesis and disproportion between the capital and the provinces have given rise to endless musings among writers. The philosophy of place is instructive. Having "ascended" to Paris, what does a writer do then? With exhilaration, he takes hold of provincial life as material for thought that he will dissect and that he will turn into his milk and honey. For provincial life conceals real life, the slow, tragic life of ordinary human beings, who, precisely for that reason, are the most human. Paris, on the other hand, rather resembles an eminence or a paroxysm that sets the tone while exposing its emptiness. The Parisian writer goes to the provinces to recharge his batteries: it is there that he finds the real life that his creativity needs. It is always said that Paris sucks all the talent out of its provinces, which never cease to produce new minds, so as to offer them anew to the capital. But the provinces also represent the breeding ground to which we always return.

This antinomy is rich in meaning. It forges, in France at least, but surely elsewhere too, the opposition that has sometimes become a confrontation between the rich and the poor, the educated and the uneducated, the center and the periphery, the cosmopolitans and rural people. Today, the confrontation between those who are "anywhere" and those who are "somewhere," which affects most Western countries, is unfolding in France between the capital and its provinces. It is enough simply to look at how Emmanuel Macron, the leading figure of the cosmopolitans, is achieving election results that are fit for a general in the districts in the center of Paris, whereas the "Yellow Vests" come from the provinces.

The antinomy here permits one to measure, in every era, the distance between tradition and modernity. What is done and thought in Paris points the way to the future of mores. What is done and said in the provinces recalls the past. It was François Mauriac who described these philosophical differences with the most precision. He showed how the anonymity of a big city sets people free, whereas in the provinces, proximity suffocates and corrupts relationships. French centralization and the preeminence over everything else that is conferred upon Paris, which he calls a "cerebral congestion,"[6] essentially allows us to gauge the scale of modernity. The remote capital, so different from its provinces, produces the most novel inventions and lives in harmony with the world. It flies away from reality itself, bypasses morality, and forgets the wisdom of nations. Only the provinces, Mauriac claims, still have a sense of right and wrong! This means that Paris is always at the forefront of moral evolution. It is the first to liberalize morals, after which the provinces follow, sometimes backward. These reflections, which are without a doubt excessive, allow us to understand the extent to which contemporary social detachments in France are related to the detachment between Paris and its provinces. It is the cosmopolitanism of Paris that gives rise to the fury of hardened people in the provinces. And the revolt is all the more bitter when the distance between the two is so great, so long-standing, and so established. Here, you have the particular, there you have the universal. And by a sort of fatality, all talents are drawn to this center like butterflies to light!

To understand France, it is necessary to take into account this intrinsic dissociation. Parisians despise; people in the provinces envy. In 1834, the German writer Heinrich Heine wrote about his trip to France: "The people whom I met in the provinces seemed to me almost like highway markers, on whose foreheads were inscribed their distance—greater or lesser—from the capital. The women there perhaps seek in Catholicism a consolation for the grief of not being able to live in Paris."[7]

8

Intellectuals

The prestige of the French intellectual begins at the very moment in which the prestige of the clergy fades. It is a matter of a substitution. It was during the eighteenth century that the power of people who think, those who played no small part in the revolution, started to increase. Théodore Zeldin remarked that, in the middle of the eighteenth century, censorship became laxer, and at the same time the prestige of men of letters grew.[1] France shares the following specificity with Russia: the influence of thinkers in everyday and political life. The two countries also share revolutionary violence. There is a link between a profound attraction for thought and the pretention to remake the world.

As was the case in Russia before the revolution of 1917, in France before 1789, the intellectuals had been, along with all of society, kept away from any political decisions by an autocratic power. They ignored the political situation and believed that it was written in books. They, thus, produced utopias that would exaggerate violence so as to bring it to fruition. Thus, autocratic power reproduces itself. French centralism, by preventing subjects from performing economic and political actions, accentuated the abstract character of speeches and debates. Intellectuals were purely speculative on this, and their glosses were chimerical. In a centralized country, a revolution more easily produces utopias: in France in 1789 and in Russia in 1917. Tocqueville's analysis in this regard is corroborated much later by Solzhenitsyn's analysis concerning Russia (in *The Red Wheel*).[2] Both here and there, the elite who had access neither to economic affairs nor to projects concerning political freedom (the administrators were not political) had to confine themselves to pure speculation, all the more because of their absolute lack of concrete reference points. They based their demands on an imaginary society. This produced ideological, and thus bloody, revolutions.

The crumbling of the people into a separate multitude, typical of all absolute powers, gives rise to a profound individualism, off of which literature feeds. The intellectual is first and foremost an "I," or, to put it more politely, a conscience. Well, these intellectuals play a crucial, and quite a precise, role in the history of French political development: in every era, they are the champions and the heralds of autocratic power.

In the eighteenth century, economists and especially philosophers were the first to question the government in order to shake it to its foundations. However, it is astonishing to see that these intellectuals had no interest in civil liberties, be they, for example, the Physiocrats or Voltaire. Generally speaking, the intellectuals in this era preferred enlightened despotism. What was important for them was the prince's competence instead of civil liberties: they were Platonists. Voltaire's adventure with Frederick the Great is very similar to Plato's with the tyrant, Dionysius of Syracuse: it was the same desire (and delusion) for the philosopher, which was to make the autocrat good so as to achieve a perfect regime. For many of them are utopians, persuaded that they could erase a tragic human past and remake a new nation. A utopia is necessarily egalitarian, and eighteenth-century France was the cradle of Soviet communism. Speaking about the intellectuals of the time, Tocqueville wrote: "Not only do they hate certain privileges, diversity itself is odious to them: they would adore equality even in servitude."[3] It is true that French thought mistrusts freedom, which it translates into anarchy and inequality.

Together with Destutt de Tracy's movement of "ideologues" (the science of ideas) at the time of the revolution, with Saint-Simon's desire to turn intellectuals into a new clergy capable of implementing a politics guided by science, with Auguste Comte or utopians such as Fourier or Proudhon, a vast current emerged at the dawn of modernity to defend a Platonic style of autocracy. The twentieth century represents the continuation of this process. Starting at the dawn of the twentieth century, the majority of French intellectuals sided either with fascism or with communism. One could cite countless examples. Naturally, there were, among them, many honest people on both sides who changed their minds once they realized the danger of the ideologies in question. But, on the whole, they did a great deal of harm. A number of them defended either Hitler or — more often — the fascisms and corporatisms of the interwar period, Mussolini or Salazar. Convinced of the dramatic decline of the West, they were expecting renewed spiritual and moral vigor from these regimes. The defeat of National Socialism in 1945 and the discovery of its crimes brought along with it the downfall of the entirety of right-wing thought, from the extreme right to the moderate right. Henceforth, just being conservative was enough to be called a Nazi and to have one's voice silenced for good. But communism, which was on the winning side, was triumphant. In France, the postwar period was the golden age of Marxism. Without any exaggeration, it could be said that in the 1970s almost all French intellectuals were Marxists of one stripe or another—Stalinists, Maoists, Trostkyites, and so on. Conservative intellectuals (Raymond Aron, Julien Freund) were rare and generally ostracized. Sartre wrote that "Marxism is the unsurpassable horizon of our time" and that "every anticommunist is a dog."[4] This was not an issue of an opinion or a conviction, but rather an ideology, one that was convinced that it alone held the truth, and, as a result, it was intolerant. The Tel Quel group, which, with Philippe Sollers, went to Maoist China in 1974 to praise the most monstrous regime of the time, and Jean Lacouture's shameful defense of the genocide in Cambodia all call to mind André Gide's trip to the USSR in 1936. At this juncture, one would be embarrassed even to speak of "intellectuals." Who are these so-called thinkers, who are incapable of the slightest Cartesian doubt, but who spend their lives lying and cheating in order to come to the aid of sinister regimes? After the Second World War, a quarter of the students at the École Normale Supérieure, the citadel of France's great minds, were members of the Communist Party. This is how Raymond Aron came to call his book *L'opium des intellectuels* [*The Opium of the Intellectuals*]: he says that French intellectuals are perpetually in search of a religion (since the erasure of Christianity) and that their unanimous Marxism combines all the characteristics of intolerance and verbal fanaticism that can be found in religions.[5] Aron's book was written in the 1960s: sixty years later, we could replace "Marxism" with "wokism."

France is a country that is particularly smitten with ideologies. It prefers ideas to reality. Tocqueville, who knew the extent to which extreme ideas are dirty bombs, described France as "the most brilliant and dangerous nation in Europe, more capable of genius than common sense."[6] The French Revolution, unlike the American Revolution, sought much less to reform the country than to create a new humanity. The French Enlightenment, unlike the American or Scottish Enlightenment, sought concrete freedom much less than triumphant reason. In France, Marxism was so entrenched that it was necessary to wait until the fall of the Berlin Wall for it to fade away: only universal ridicule could put an end to it, but certainly not the lucidity of our brilliant brains. The 1981 election campaign was still dominated by the "Common Program," a memorial to farcical Marxism.

The French Revolution resembled a religious revolution, in that it aimed at regenerating the human condition far more than at replacing a dynasty or a government. With the French Revolution, we probably have before our eyes the birth of what one would later call an ideology: a kind of immanent religion, a religion on account of its eschatological and fanatical aspect, immanent because happiness on earth replaces Christian salvation. The year 1789 will produce 1917. It will be remembered that Lenin and Trotsky constantly compared their actions to those of the protagonists in 1789. But it is necessary to go much further: France, in the twentieth century, with its ideological proselytizing, has educated many of the world's tyrants, and the most bloodthirsty at that. Pol Pot, to name but one, was educated by Parisian communism. In the words of the postwar philosopher Georges Gusdorf, France created the figure of the "philanthropist-terrorist."[7]

At the turn of the twentieth century, lonely left-wing intellectuals gradually transformed their Marxism into cultural leftism one the one hand and into ecologism on the other hand. It still is an issue of ideologies, which are threatening and intolerant pseudoreligions. They produce new censors who abuse and ostracize. The tendency of the French intellectual is this aspiration to become a guru, to dominate power with mind, which can even lead to a predominant influence, such as when Bernard-Henri Lévy persuaded Nicolas Sarkozy to undertake the war in Libya; and the disastrous consequences of that are well known.

Solzhenitsyn has clearly shown how both the French and Russian revolutions were prepared, nurtured, and inspired by intellectuals (*The Red Wheel; Revolution et mensonge*). In both countries, both equally centralized and deprived of intermediary governing bodies, thinkers were ideologues who were less worried about conquering freedoms than about re-creating human reality—that is, making utopias real; hence, the terror on both sides. The fact that France has, in every era, nurtured cohorts of ideological or totalitarian intellectuals is not a trivial characteristic, like a certain taste for food or for the opera. It is a trait that responds to the rest: to a political system of Platonic obedience, in which thinking from on high is done for the immature people. Today, when France is governed by Emmanuel Macron, a typical young recruit of the republican mandarinate, you will not find a salon in Paris where they do not whisper: "The people know nothing, we have to make decisions for them." Ideological moments (the revolutionary period at the end of the eighteenth century or the Marxist period in the twentieth century) are merely the excesses of this national inclination.

9

The Right and the Left

Some commentators and analysts today have a tendency to claim that the divide between left and right is obsolete, that it no longer makes sense. I absolutely deny this assertion, and I am going to show why. I believe that this polarity is essential in all Western countries.

Why is the right-left divide still valid? It is because it corresponds to the historical development of Western countries. It is worth noting that this divide did not exist before the revolution. So, why is it necessary now? It is because, in all of our countries, the revolutionary epoch opened the modern era as a period of historical emancipation. One can say that, previously, emancipation had been silent and very slow, linked more to evangelical demands than to historical imperatives. Starting with the revolutionary epoch and going forward, a demand for emancipation appeared and developed: progress. It was in the nineteenth century that slavery was abolished, and in the twentieth century that women became emancipated. The right and the left were born of the demands of this movement. Is it necessary to emancipate many people and very quickly? This is the left. Is it sometimes unwise, useless, or even perverse to emancipate? This is the right. The opposition between the two poles never ends, because emancipation itself has no end, even if it takes on different forms. It is therefore a question of historical evolution, which appears in Western peoples because, as Jan Patočka put it, these people, at the very advent of modernity, exit from prehistory "like a captivity carried out in the amity of the gods"[1] in order to enter into living history, in which they attempt to give meaning and direction to the world—hence, the polemical and tragic nature of history, because giving direction triggers debates and fights.

The entire history of the twentieth century as a "European civil war" (Ernst Nolte), as a barbaric struggle to the death between communism and Nazism, is a struggle between the left and the right, each of them extremist and corrupted. And it is difficult to believe that we can now move on from this cleavage, simply because history is not over (contrary to the claims of a few false prophets) and because we are still bogged down in the tragic question of how far emancipation should go, and at what speed. Today, those who assert that they stand apart from this debate adopt either de Gaulle's attitude, by claiming, on account of their superior position, to stand outside of it because they are attached only to a definitive common good, or a monarchical attitude, as in the case of Emmanuel Macron; or they defend a technocratic consensus (this is the attitude of most leaders in institutional Europe), one founded upon a liberal-pragmatic economic belief that professes to have no adversary insofar as it claims to encompass all of reality. In both cases, the attitude is antidemocratic.

The right stands for rootedness, while the left stands for emancipation. A thousand nuances exist, but the essence is still there. Right-wing thought emphasizes what precedes us, be it history or culture. It sees us as each having deep roots in time and space. We depend on our biological and spiritual ancestors. We depend on the land of our birth and are located within landscapes. The right is conservative and does not wish to detach individuals from their origins, on which individuals are always dependent. It tends to believe that the future will not necessarily be more attractive than the past. So, it shies away from change. Not believing that the present is always happy or a fortiori perfect, it accepts the finitude and tragedy of the human world, often in terms of a religious spirit; it believes in the *human condition*, and, as such, it considers it to be hubris to profess to change the course of it. Left-wing thinking believes in human progress, which unfolds as successive emancipations: we can liberate man from a certain number of servitudes that stem from history, prejudice, and habit. It is a question of deconstructing the prejudices on which societies are often based, in order to liberate individuals and make them happier. The left sees humans as more undifferentiated, more malleable, and more capable of renovation and reinvention. In this respect, it draws from Pico della Mirandola (man is an animal without essence, capable of becoming anything) and from Sartre (existence precedes and makes essence). The Belgian historian Léo Moulin presents it in this way: the right believes in original sin, while the left tends to be Pelagian (from Pelagius, the fifth-century Breton monk who believed that human freedom could erase original sin).[2] For Rousseau and Engels, evil appears in history within evil structures (property, marriage, the state), and could therefore disappear with the disappearance of these structures.

Naturally, everything depends on where one draws the limits between what needs to be changed, what can be changed, and what should not and cannot be changed. All the variants exist. The discussion about medically aided reproduction, or on any other question of transhumanism, separates the conservative right, which fears giving rise to monstrosities, and the progressive left, which defends new emancipations.

And, of course, each of the ways of seeing has its own corruptions, which sow wars and horrors in our history, for each
person is capable of engendering true ideologies, which are
closed systems ready for totalitarianism. The corruption of the
right is the veneration of the past as such and the radical refusal
of change—that is, even a desire to go backward. The corruption of the left is the adoration of progress as movement, to the
point at which any stability becomes slavery, from which we
must continually free ourselves—something Leon Trotsky calls
"life in the bivouac."[3]

The extreme left thinks that we can reinvent our condition—
for example, change our sex if ours does not suit us. The extreme
right believes that nothing should change because the human
condition is there as an essence and that, for example, the roles
of men and women are fixed by nature. The extreme right, at work
in Germany as a romantic nation and deployed in Nazism after
the "conservative revolution," freezes itself in the roots that it
considers as historical and that it brandishes as dogma. The extreme left, at work in the Soviet Union with communism, professes to rewrite the human condition and the entirety of nature,
and it freezes the "bivouac" in dogma. Both use terror to succeed,
because in both cases, it is a question of impossible projects,
the work of mad scientists. No one can set the past in stone, no
one can remake humanity from the ground up. Every episode in
human history, beginning with modern times, has been a debate
between rootedness and emancipation.

In France, as in every Western country in the modern era,
this cleavage took on a sui generis form. In France, the revolutionary era, at the end of the eighteenth century, produced, for
the first time, a left-wing current that demanded the emancipation of the Third Estate and its participation in power and that
voted to end the privileges of the nobility. And then, the episode
with Napoleon is more complex: it represented a power on the
right insofar as it defended order, yet he conquered for the cause

of the Enlightenment. That being said, Napoleon ushered in the tradition in France of what would be called the Bonapartist right wing, which presupposed a charismatic leader and an authoritarian power. Various currents of the right wing followed one another in the nineteenth and then the twentieth century. The book edited by Jean-François Sirinelli enumerates them: counterrevolutionary, legitimizer, Orleanist, Bonapartist, liberal, revolutionary, fascist, and extremist.[4] As for the left, it produced all kinds of Jacobin and socialist currents throughout the nineteenth century, right up to communism and socialism in the twentieth century.

In the twentieth century, between the two wars, France experienced a period in which the right was powerful, but the country as a whole was dominated by left-wing thinking. The right-wing currents of the interwar period, close to the spirit of the German conservative revolution, quickly turned to fascism, and at some points flirted with Nazism, and, thus, lost their reputation for good after the Second World War. General de Gaulle was a typical right-wing figure (a reader of Maurras and Bernanos), but above all he was an autocrat who placed himself above parties and divisions and succeeded in making emancipatory political decisions (such as the independence of Algeria) so as to make people forget that he was right-wing. François Mitterrand is a typical right-wing man (a reader of Maurras and Bernanos!), but he joined the Socialist Party because there was no future elsewhere, and throughout his political career he managed to forget or deny that he was awarded the "Francisque," an award from the Vichy regime. So, the whole political problem in France after 1945 had been not to be right-wing, or at least not to appear so. During this period, the Socialists were not always in power—far from it—but they were in complete control of culture, and until the fall of the Berlin Wall, most French intellectuals were left-wing, while the others would not say so. In fact, until the turn of the century, the term *right-wing* was not used: it was not politically correct. If you were elected on the right, you would call yourself an "independent" or a "centrist." A party with a right-wing temperament would never call itself right-wing; it would call itself Gaullist or independent. The term reappeared in the first decade of the present century.

In France, as in the majority of other Western countries, right-wing currents have been redeployed and strengthened since the turn of the century. This is due, certainly, to the final defeat of communism after the fall of the Berlin Wall and the shared feeling that true socialism was the greatest scam of the century. Moreover, Western socialists have not succeeded in proposing policies that are both divorced from communist totalitarianism and viable in a normal world, which is, for us Westerners, a politically liberal world. Socialism is a chemically unstable product; there is no liberal Marxism, which is an oxymoron. In addition, France is already a country that is so socialist in itself, on account of its Colbertism and its highly developed social redistribution, that an even more socialistic program would bring it dangerously close to Sovietism. But then, ambient liberalism at the international level and in its European instances has exploited the French mindset, which is not very inclined toward liberalism. Thanks to Europe, the country is now in the process of emerging from its socialist encumbrance, albeit with pain: to hear trade union leaders and many political figures tell it, we are being governed in an ultraliberal manner. This is stunning when one sees the state constraints that are deployed everywhere, and more so than in any other developed country.

What is interesting is the shift of intellectual currents since the turn of the century. Immediately after the fall of the Berlin Wall, French intellectuals little by little abandoned their lingering Marxism, which took many forms. They broadly became conservative, a transition made easy by the fact that the ecological current, which is highly influential, quite frankly is conservative. However, they are not liberals, except for a small handful of them who are quite marginalized. One could say that there is no liberal current in France, even though the intellectual force that was Marxist in the 1980s, with Foucault and Derrida, is now conservative. This does not mean that it has become easy to call oneself right-wing. Most of these intellectuals, who were left-wing until the turn of the century, are hesitant to call themselves right-wing, even though they are often quite conservative and, in some cases, reactionary. If Gramsci is to be believed, the development of a powerful intellectual current sets the stage, in the medium term, for governments of the same hue—François Mitterrand's accession to power in 1981 had been made possible as a consequence of the intellectual domination of the left since 1945. But, for now, one cannot see any movement toward the beginning of a conservative politics. Right-wing politicians are too often bland or corrupt, and they lack the courage of their convictions. However, programs that are both liberal and conservative, while not claiming to be so, are spreading and taking shape. With the development of globalization, France can no longer live like the "closed commercial state" of which Fichte spoke. It cannot do anything other than face up to the onslaught of competition. It must be remembered that when François Mitterrand came to power, he could not find any better option than reducing the amount of money each French citizen was allowed to take out of the country—a protocommunist measure designed to close the country in on itself. Today, this has become absolutely impossible, and we can measure the changes that have been produced by this. On other fronts, and in particular on the so-called societal front, many of the prejudices of the left are dead and buried together with their failures. The left has stopped lauding divorce and promoting disastrous school methods based on the so-called innate autonomy of the child. The hackneyed argument for the notorious "French exception," which consisted in boasting of exceptional dominance in all sectors, has fizzled out. We are now realizing that the pay-as-one-goes pension system

impoverishes a country when it has to endure both unemployment and demographic decline. The points-based pension system, which in the past was ardently championed by a few small
groups of liberals who were alone in the world, is now having an
impact. All of this demonstrates the eruption of reality in a country that has just spent more than half a century gnawing away at
Marxist ideologies. It is lamentable that these measures are dictated solely by economic necessity, rather than by fundamental
beliefs—and this provokes resentment and rebellion.

10

The People and the Elite

It will be remembered that when Lenin came to power, he was convinced of having the people on his side: What could be more natural, given that he desired only their good? So, he proclaimed a democracy and played along, only to discover very quickly that, while hopes for the downfall of the regime were well shared among the population, opinions about the positive goals to be pursued differed. When he saw that the proletarians aspired to create trade unions rather than the "bright future" of Marxism, he was convinced that he was the victim of high treason, and he immediately abandoned democracy.

What is happening to us today in the West is not very different, and France is equally affected by this process, as are other countries. At the turn from the twentieth century to the twenty-first, intellectuals on the left realized that the working classes were abandoning them. For a number of reasons—because the left's struggle seemed obsolete after the end of communism, or maybe because there was no longer a "proletariat" in the Marxist sense—the impoverished working classes started to vote for the right—nay, even for the extreme right. The political and intellectual left was convinced that it was the victim of high treason. No longer was the choice one of being in a trade union versus *brighter future*, rather, as was stated during the crisis of the Yellow Vests, the issue was "worrying about the end of the month instead of worrying about the end of the world." And yet there is a coriaceous link between these two quips: then and now, concrete, realistic ends are valued as opposed to vaguely eschatological expectations that are more snobbish than true. Foreshadowed by Lenin a century ago, the contemporary scene is here in its entirety.

The crucial question that David Goodhart raises in *The Road to Somewhere: The Populist Revolt and the Future of Politics* affects France and other Western countries. It is a sociological question that becomes a social and then an ideological one.

First of all, it is sociological insofar as it concerns the logical consequences of globalization for the social fabric and for behavior. From the moment in which it becomes so easy to travel and communicate between continents, the upper social classes adopt the whole world for their country. They intermarry, speak several languages, and maintain residences in several capitals. In this way, they increasingly differentiate themselves from the working class, who move little and have no idea about the world beyond their own province. This difference that is both sociological and cultural difference is quickly becoming a social one. The two classes that confront each other are no longer the bourgeoisie and proletariat, as was the case a century ago, but the nomadic and the sedentary, because the appropriation of space is the pinnacle of culture, just as the appropriation of time once was.

The French upper classes are, thus, as uninterested in France as the eighteenth-century nobles who spent their lives at the court of Versailles were in their provinces. They see the national sphere as too small and outdated. They compare their country to others, and not always in a favorable light. Of all the countries in the Organisation for Economic Co-operation and Development (OECD), France has the strongest link between children's academic success and the gentrification of their parents: it is indeed a form of class warfare. However, this is no longer set up on a purely economic and cultural plane, but on an ideological one— the elites no longer despise people simply because they lack codes and customs, but because they are backward-looking, xenophobic, and even racist.

This new differentiation still reflects that of right and left. It is the contemporary version of the debate between the right and the left. The right is rooted in its culture, its identity, and its territories, and consequently looks down on immigration. The left is emancipated from its globalist identities and wants to live in an open world in which all cultures live together. The "somewhere" is today's right, the "anywhere" is today's left. The traditional distinction has been adapted to fit in with globalization. The difference from a century ago is that the people are no longer on the left, but instead on the right.

France is a country that, since 1793, has easily succumbed to violent ideologies, and the political battles around them are ferocious, with their insults and even ostracism, at least compared to political battles in neighboring countries where partisan speech is freer. Debate is thus easily transformed into an aggressive rejection of the right, quickly described as extreme right-wing for the purposes of the battle. The taboos of political correctness are in full force. France is much more sensitive to political correctness than, for example, Italy, where practically anything can be said or debated—the writer Marc Bloch saw a link here with the cult of form that is so French: "Our press, almost all of it, and everything that is fundamentally academic in our literature, have spread the cult of convenience, in my opinion."[1]

The cultural left in France is no longer widely in the majority like it was forty years ago, but it has nevertheless remained intolerant, as can be seen from the woke people who are the heirs of conquering Marxism. For example, the newly created television channel CNews, which initiates hitherto nonexistent conservative and right-wing media, stirs up the fury of left-wing currents that cannot bear to see their monopoly taken away. There are times when some conservatives cry totalitarianism. But I always become angry when I hear the word "totalitarian" used in connection with political correctness and other things—because I believe that it is necessary not to hammer on words by using them indiscriminately; otherwise they will become useless for their intended purpose.

The illusion of having gotten rid of the left-right divide and the obsession with conformist thought together produce a denial of democracy that is at the same time a denial of politics. President Macron claims that he is neither left nor right, but that he controls all the different levers of the problems and works only for the common good. This is very Gaullist, monarchist, and technocratic—it is a fraud, because no man is God and everyone has his preferences, which are more straightforward if you state them. Emmanuel Macron has organized his government as an antidemocracy: he has no adversaries because he is both right and left. He has only one enemy: the far right. And all his electoral campaigns tend to show that we must vote for him, since he alone is the one facing Satan (he calls his enemy "leprosy"). This has nothing to do with democracy, which is a debate between adversaries about the embodiment of the common good.

11

French Secularism

Secularism is a specifically French affair. Yet it represents only a national expression of secularization, a Western phenomenon that is shared by all Western countries (that is, if one does not consider Israel to be a Western country—Israel is a theocracy). It is necessary to begin by explaining what secularization is before addressing secularism.

Political power begins to separate itself from religious power in ancient Greece as early as the seventh century BCE, with the creation of the archonship in Athens. This reform consisted in the separation of political government, held by two archons, from religious government, left solely to the ancient king. The distinction between the two orders was conceptualized by Aristotle, who describes politics as an imperfect art, the work of mere mortals, and without any link to the sacred. When Christianity comes to these regions to proclaim its message, the very existence of transcendence makes secularization possible and legitimates it. The distance between the human and the divine is such that politics cannot take over what is sacred along with everything else: a separation is necessary (Islam, which is also a religion of transcendence, will give rise to theocracies, but by erasing political power). Christianity will therefore grant specific legitimacy to each of the two powers, within its own sphere. It is a case of "Render unto Caesar what is Caesar's and unto God what is God's," while at the same time denying Christ's pursuit of earthly royalty. All of this is nothing surprising given the mindset of the time, which was accustomed to such a distinction (recall the revolt of Alexander the Great's officers when, while emulating the Asian kings he met along the way, he tried to force them to prostrate themselves before him).

Subsequently, the Christian kingdoms of Europe experienced forms of theocracy, as under the Carolingians, but it was not long before a body of thought developed that conceptualized the separation of orders. Thomas Aquinas defended Aristotle's belief that politics is a strictly human affair. In the fourteenth century, William of Ockham and Marsilius of Padua set down the pillars for what was to become the theory of secularization. They conceptually legitimated the separation of orders and described attempts at theocracy (in particular, papal attempts to govern princes) as errors contrary to the true faith.

In France, specifically, the secularization that was characteristic of the European continent, and then of the West as a whole, was to become secularism.

In order to understand this specificity, it is necessary to understand the ramifications of the various modern revolutions. The first three (Dutch, English, and American) took place in Protestant countries. The fourth (French) took place in a Catholic country. Protestantism straight away accepted the political and social modernity that was brought about by the revolutions, whereas Catholicism vigorously rejected this modernity throughout the nineteenth century. In France, this situation produced the need to erase religion as much as possible so as to be able to develop modern reforms. For France, the Enlightenment was tantamount to atheism, whereas for America and the United Kingdom, the Enlightenment meant an emancipation rooted in religion; and this changes everything.

As opposed to what happens in Protestant countries, in France, political power cannot get along with a religion that a priori contests that power, and even less is it able to integrate it, let alone to include it.

The French Revolution was waged against both the nobility and the clergy—in other words, against both governing estates. The fervor of eighteenth-century French intellectuals and of the revolutionaries of 1789 against Catholicism did not reflect a rejection of religion, but a rejection of the power of clerics. As Tocqueville clearly showed, the church was attacked for its political and social activities, because of its roles as an owner and as an administrator.[1] But that is not all: the church was rejected, and France would spend the nineteenth century doing everything in its power to rein in Catholicism, which was still wholly in charge of schools and health care until the 1905 Separation Act. "Their instinct tells them that the only thing preventing them from being rich and happy is theology," said Proudhon.[2] France is indeed "the eldest daughter of the church," according to an old adage that goes back to the baptism of Clovis. But it is also the eldest daughter of an atheistic and ideological revolution, which will have descendants in Russia and the other communist countries. For France, it was a duty of emancipation to fight against Christianity (it was because women went to church too much that they gained the right to vote only quite late). France has the habit of reducing the church to its Inquisition. With the hundreds of millions of deaths of the twentieth century that are due to two atheistic ideologies, France still considers religion to be the real villain of history.

One could ask the question—which is beyond the scope of this essay—whether or not France is the only country in the West to have had such a difficult time putting up with the old powers of Catholicism. In any case, the situation today is the following: France is, along with with the Czech Republic, the most nonreligious country in Europe. One possible explanation cites the violence of the wars of religion in these two countries (the persecution of the Hussites in Bohemia and the persecution of Protestants in France). The facts are there.

Distrust vis-à-vis religion is a constant in France. Let us consider two stories separated by a century. Jean Jaurès allowed his daughter to receive First Communion: attacked by the socialist press and obligated to defend himself, he did so with a clumsiness that humiliated him anew. In 2001, Régis Debray, a former communist, had his son baptized: he received the same taunts and reproaches that had not changed in a century. He had to write an op-ed piece in *Le Monde* in order to vindicate himself.

French secularism calls for tolerance for all currents of thought, on the condition that they do not stem from jejune roots and are not overly permeated with conservatism. For a long time, patriotism was judged as being Vichy-ist (that is, supportive of Pétain's government) and unsavory, even if things are slowly beginning to change in this respect. Religion is tolerated, as long as it is not flaunted, remains buried deep in one's heart, and refrains from expressing itself. It is not forbidden, of course, but it is hounded ironically. In a public high school, few Christian children dare admit that they go to mass: it is frowned upon.

As for me, I believe that keeping traditional religions hidden will not lead to widespread atheism or agnosticism, as is the wish of the militant, secular French, but rather to the attachment to other religions or pseudoreligions. Atheism is an intellectual posture and, therefore, something that is rare and insecure. Human beings have an intrinsic need to seek out mysteries, because they know that they have to die and do not know the meaning of their existence. It is a mistake not to want to recognize that. A free country is not a country without religion, but a country in which temporal and spiritual powers are separated by secularization—the worst thing of all is a tyranny of the clergy, regardless of their denomination.

For many reasons, French secularism today is a concept that barely needs to be justified anymore. First, because it arose during an era when power and a powerful church battled for influence. It arose during an era when it was generally believed that scientific progress was going to render religions obsolete: the sciences would answer every metaphysical question, or so it was naively thought. Convinced of the obsolescence of religions, certain countries, such as the Soviet Union and France, coordinated their disappearance, and then were contradicted by the facts: as soon as bans were lifted, religions reappeared like flowers in spring. But the second reason that makes the concept of secularism archaic is the transformation of French society, which is henceforth obligated to take into account a growing and powerful Islam, financed from outside and prospering from our guilt. It is becoming ridiculous and counterproductive to extol secularism as a way of keeping religions under wraps when a triumphant Islam ironically occupies our streets, schools, and beaches. It is a pleasure to see that for decades we have done everything to ensure that the Catholic diet on Fridays has no effect on our school cafeterias, whereas today we feel obligated to respect the Muslim diet there. Lastly, today's secularism in no way serves agnostic tolerance, as it had always claimed to be doing. It serves for the expansion of the only religion that mocks its proclamations and takes advantage of its situation as a former victim.

I conclude that "secularism," the specifically French heir to Western secularization, today requires a serious overhaul, a readaptation to the exigencies of the times.

12

The Present State of Religion

Today, in France, what does Catholicism, which is traditionally the country's dominant religion, represent?

The first half of the twentieth century in France was dominated by the thought of Charles Maurras. One will never understand the extent to which his thought actually contributed to the toppling of the religion that it claimed to serve. Maurrasisme is a modern form of Machiavellianism. Religion is an instrument through which power is bolstered by means of the moral and behavioral discipline that it encourages. We have known this for a long time: a strong religion prevents power from becoming too strong. Maurras was agnostic. He held that religious beliefs were for the weak-minded—children, women, and fools. Until the Second World War, this school of thought enjoyed a decisive influence and it produced obvious results: if religion is a pleasant tale that serves only to bind society together, it will fade away at the first opportunity. If it is only a facade, then it is held together only with paint. Maurrasisme triggered the agnosticism that it secretly nurtured. In the second half of the twentieth century, Marxism took the place of religion for intellectuals, while Catholicism suffered terribly. The church was rattled by crises and intellectual heresies (Marx and Lacan were studied in seminaries instead of Saint Thomas Aquinas). Of course, for many, the calling as well as the practice was lost. A sweeping current of left-wing Catholics, who, as they put it, had hoped "to walk partway with Marxism," had abandoned religion before Marxism. Ultimately, at the end of the century, we found ourselves in the situation ironically described by Woody Allen: "God is dead, Marx is dead, [Lenin is dead], and I don't feel so good either."

The fall of the Berlin Wall and the final communist letdowns coincided with the end of the Thirty Glorious Years, the end of a cycle of economic ease, and the end of illusions of uninterrupted progress. Perhaps it was this return to reality at the turn of the century that gave rise to upheavals in French Catholic sociology, which became significantly younger. The generation of children of baby boomers, whose parents had done their utmost to pass on nothing, gave rise to the generation of World Youth Days, John Paul II, and new missions. Where were these young people able to find what no one wanted to pass on to them? The fact remains that the massive rallies of "Manif-pour-tous" ["Protest-for-All"] to resist the introduction of marriage between two people of the same sex revealed the existence in France of a constellation of numerous and fervent young Christians, whereas previously religious practice had long seemed reserved for the elderly. The demonstrations revealed this constellation to itself, so to speak, and soon afterwards it set about creating all sorts of associations — religious, cultural, political, and charitable — that abound today. These Christians of the early twenty-first century are the opposite of the Maurrasians of a century ago, and the opposite of the left-wing Catholics of half a century ago. Their religion is anything but sociological. They go to mass not out of tradition (as we used to say between the wars, a century ago: "I am a churchgoer, just not a believer"), but rather because they have faith. Since the May 1968 era witnessed the removal of kneelers in churches, people now kneel on the flagstones, which is impressive to see. They raise their children in the faith and take part in all kinds of religious activities. In some Parisian parishes, young Catholics regularly gather in the streets in the evenings to evangelize. I know this kind of practice might seem banal to an American. But in France, it is completely new and unexpected.

That being said, these groups are not numerous. But they count because they are active and because they are in the process of supplanting the old communist elite. Forty years ago, the top students among the graduates of the elite Grandes Écoles were Stalinists or Trotskyites. Today, it is not unusual for the best to be young, well-educated, and enterprising Christians. It needs to be said that in France Catholicism persisted in the families of the elite: whereas in the past Catholicism was the religion of the peasants, today it is the religion of the most educated families. Hervé Le Bras and Emmanuel Todd, who are not under suspicion of any particular sympathy toward French Catholicism, glean from their sociological surveys the ability of Catholic families to withstand the educational and social crisis in comparison with individualist-decomposed-recomposed families.[1] An elite is forming in this crucible.

Moreover, what does not help prevent Catholicism from having lost and still losing many of its assets and from being a religion in constant decline is the fact that the percentage of children enrolled in catechism classes continues to fall and is now practically at a bare minimum. In a general way, Catholicism is becoming a culture, and we know that the transformation of a cult into a culture is not a good sign for the religion in question. It means that it has been desacralized, that people have ceased to believe in it, so to speak, and that its expressions have been transformed into rituals or myths in the form of tales. Jesus has become a mythical figure symbolizing beautiful virtue, like the Buddha. So, in many Christian schools, a history of religions course has replaced the catechism. Western countries, having lost their original religions, live by principles that are derived from those religions but that they adapt to their own tastes (Chesterton spoke of Christian truths gone mad, such as human rights and their avatars). Ancient beliefs become aesthetic or moralizing myths. The "disenchantment of the world" (Max Weber) is not definitive!

So, these young Catholics remain a minority, albeit an active one, and they have to practice the "ketman"—that is, keeping their convictions hidden, in certain cases, in the face of the power of correct thought that tries to embarrass them. I am thinking, for example, of the topic of in-vitro fertilization being included on the national high school examinations, which has made it clear that some students had to lie about their convictions or risk failing the exam. For it is necessary to note that these groups are intentionally conservative, whether environmentalist or not, which is of course something quite novel with respect to their parents or grandparents.

So, at the religious level, we are heading toward a society in which Marxist atheism is replaced, in one respect, by Islam, and in another respect by young Catholics, both of whom are determined and enterprising. The sociology of each one is very different. Islam has the advantage of being beloved by the media and of always being right, so to speak, because of colonialist guilt. Catholics have the advantage of belonging to the educated elite and of having a very long history of underhanded persecution behind them. But it is difficult to imagine that Islam can thrive in a country like France, which is so committed to emancipation. The sustained support given to Islam by some of our intellectuals is such a flagrant contradiction that it has become ironic. How can we simultaneously publicize Me Too and argue in favor of the Islamic veil? Michel Houellebecq's book *Soumission* [Submission] aptly describes the tortuous, hypocritical path we could end up traversing from the Enlightenment's atheism to Islam, haunted by our own guilt, a kind of redemptive self-flagellation. But this is barely credible. It is hard to imagine that French women of North African origin, who have only just acquired their freedom, would willingly (and masochistically?) give in to the captivity offered them by Islam.

Naturally, branches of Christianity that are perhaps more suited to the present world are developing here as elsewhere: evangelicalism. And branches more suited to critiques of the present world: Orthodoxy. But what is spreading the most, or easiest, in the vacuum left by modern atheism, are new wisdoms, wild theologies, and substitute religions such as Freemasonry and cults. At a time when ecology is on the way to becoming the most popular and intolerant religion, worshipers of Gaia, the cult of the Nordic gods, and so on are multiplying—a curious mix of renewed paganism and contemporary ecology. But the two are not far apart. It is not uncommon for ecology to become, in the hands of its followers, a kind of pantheism. One can think back to the pantheism controversy that Jacobi initiated right after the revolution; he saw atheism being succeeded by Spinozism. In a brief and brilliant chapter of *Democracy in America*, Tocqueville predicted that the religion of democracy would be pantheism, because all living beings are equal. And here we are; this trend is visible in France as elsewhere. It can be seen that the Enlightenment did not lead us to a triumphant and peaceful atheism, but to a search for substitute religions, essentially toward Asian wisdoms and toward pantheism.

And so, the new religious conflicts are between supporters of transcendence and those of paganism.

It is important to underline the role of French Catholics in the fight against so-called societal reforms affecting marriage, the family, and filiation. In recent years in most Western countries, these reforms have passed—even though some people are reluctant or opposed—without civil society expressing any level of criticism or rejection. In Canada, for example, marriage between two people of the same sex passed through the intermediary of judges without a democratic vote and without a stir. France is perhaps the country in which opponents have protested most vigorously, without, however, being greater in number than elsewhere in terms of percentage of the population. This is a peculiarity worth talking about.

What we call Christendom—that is, the societies in which Christianity, qua sole prescriber, inspired laws, behavior, and morals—no longer exists. Christendom, which dates back some sixteen hundred years (it was at the end of the fourth century that Christian power began to inspire laws), has faded away, and this is a considerable collapse. When our countries ask themselves questions about bioethical or transhumanist laws, they consult ethics committees on which some Christians are represented, as well as Muslims, Freemasons, Marxists, atheists, and so forth. In other words, common morality is inspired by a cultural melting pot, and no longer by Christianity, as was still the case half a century ago. This does not mean that Christianity has disappeared, but it is in the minority and has little influence. However, the energy and fervor of its followers in France stands out, because they are constantly at the forefront of opposition to these laws. The protests in 2013, despite the government's efforts to discourage and minimize them, brought together nearly a million people in Paris each time. This conveys the enormous mobilization of a community that largely remains a minority.

There is no doubt that these young Christians will remain a minority, acting as God's secret agents in society. Today, one senses, here as well as elsewhere, the extent to which "pagan" currents, nurtured by ecology, are on the rise. Ecology is unquestionably the great religion of the coming century, and its status as a natural religion encourages the worship of nature. Our contemporaries are ready for this in every country in the West, and thus in France, too.

13

The Sense of Identity and Immigration

In 2019, sociologist Jérôme Fourquet published a book with the revealing title *L'archipel français: Naissance d'une nation multiple et divisée* [The French archipelago: The birth of a multifaceted and divided nation]. In it, one finds a confirmation, in facts and figures, of what we have been feeling for years: this republican country, haunted by the idea of its unity, is in the process of crumbling into multiple communities that contradict and stand as an insult to its plan. It is necessary to comprehend what has happened.

France is a republican country, as was mentioned above. It is haunted by the idea of its unity. It unified its provinces by forcibly banning particular languages and dialects. It centralizes because it likes uniformity and equality.

What's more, France has been a country of immigration for two centuries, as the media like to say; and they are right. We have received and welcomed all sorts of nationalities, in any case, since the nineteenth century, be they Poles in the second half of the nineteenth century or Italians just after the Second World War, along with many others. This is due to the fact that we are a free, wealthy, and enviable country, accustomed to protecting our compatriots and properly welcoming those who seek refuge. This is also due to the fact that we were powerful colonizers in the nineteenth and twentieth centuries. When the inhabitants of North African countries learn and speak fluent French because it is the language of the colonizer, at the time when fractures emerge (decolonization, independence, then economic depression in the formerly colonized country), it is obvious that these inhabitants will look for work, preferably in the former metropolis whose language they speak. Similarly, it is no coincidence that Indian expatriate volunteers choose the United Kingdom.

All this makes it such that France has a mixed population, and it is not at all uncommon for French people to know of close ancestors who come from another country, European or otherwise. The country is a gateway, a central geographical point in Europe, large enough and sparsely populated enough for people to find their place here. In short, its doors have always been open. The foreigners that have been welcomed have always ended up integrating here, after periods of acceptance and adaptation that sometimes were difficult.

In a republican country like France, it no longer is a question of accepting one form or another of communitarianism, a multicultural society in which diverse groups each live in their own neighborhoods according to their own customs and perhaps even their own laws. That is what has happened with historical waves of immigration: we integrate, perhaps even assimilate, but we are not satisfied just to add on or amass. New arrivals must adapt to the culture of France, which otherwise would no longer deserve the name of republic. However, the ability to assimilate depends above all on the difference between the culture of the host and that of the immigrants. The reception of Poles, Italians, Spaniards, or Portuguese was always the reception of Christians who were carrying with them a European culture and nourished by classics that are also ours. The question became a conundrum when it was necessary to receive Arab-Muslims, who were endowed with a religion, a language, and a culture wholly different from ours.

This difficulty, from which we are still far from extricating ourselves, has given rise to a story in two chapters.

After the decolonization of the Maghreb and Africa, immigration from these countries was sizable. First of all, at France's request (in the Pompidou years), a large number of people came to work in our factories: they stayed for a few years and sent money back to their families who stayed at home. They were advantageous for French companies because they asked for less in terms of wages. Then family reunification was authorized (Chirac's government in 1976), which was all the same from an ethical point of view. This law experienced all kinds of vicissitudes. The fact remains that, from that time onward, France saw a large number of Muslims step onto its soil. It should be noted that, at the same time, Asians also entered, driven away by the communist wars in former French Indochina. However, Asians are extraordinarily adaptable and create few problems, basically being able to become part of the community without anyone noticing. This was to become another problem with the Muslims of North Africa. The culture of these new arrivals was very different from ours. I remember the public housing estate in Oyonnax (an industrial town in central-eastern France) at around 9 a.m. in those years, and all the baskets hanging from the windows: the women were locked in all day by their husbands and used to ask the social workers, or coordinators, in this way, for what they might be lacking from outside. France, true to its calling, provided all the necessary means. This was during the Thirty Glorious Years, and there was no shortage of resources.

Public housing estates were built. The people living there were helped by numerous social and cultural services that functioned as an administrative interface, were advised on children's schooling, and were offered educational leisure activities and literacy courses for adults and children alike, and so on. In other words, everything was done to achieve true integration. It is fair to say that this endeavor was initially successful: most of the young people from these families found their place in French society, as can be seen, for example, in Alice Zeniter's autobiographical book *L'art de perdre* [*The Art of Losing*].

But what happened next? French society changed from the 1980s onward. As the opulence of the Thirty Glorious Years waned and unemployment rose, the mindset became increasingly materialistic and less republican. Schools became more segmented and less successful. So, immigrant children from the suburbs did worse in school and had difficulty finding work. Governments believed that any problem could be solved with infusions of subsidies. More and more money started to be injected into immigrant neighborhoods, money sent from afar and with a kind of indifference. This, of course, was useless, since a population struggling to assimilate needs, above all, to work together with supportive people, not functionaries who just dole out cash. The immigrant population felt disrespected and experienced a kind of ostracism that left them stuck in a sad setting, with rotten schools for their children, from which they would never be able to escape. Their children began to destroy sports facilities and public places, and then began to sell drugs because there was no work for them.

It can be said that the French immigration problem does not concern the fact that a flood of immigrants has been entering the country in recent years, as is the case in Greece, Italy, or Germany. This is not the case: we receive around two hundred thousand immigrants a year, which is not enormous given the demand. The specific problem is as follows: while the first and even second generations of immigrants were integrated, their grandchildren are, so to speak, in the process of dis-integrating, for all sorts of political, economic, social, and cultural reasons. Whereas the previous generation of Arab-Muslims in France were secularized, today they have a tendency to return to traditional and radical Islam, so as to regain a lost identity. This shows that a certain number of them do not feel identified with France. The terrorism of Islamists represents the extreme tip of this trend, as do the departures of young French people to Syria in recent years. At the same time, racist and delinquent behavior is on the increase, to the point where the authorities are overwhelmed. Jewish families in the Seine-Saint-Denis region have withdrawn their children from public schools due to virulent anti-Semitism on the part of young Muslims. The loss of control over "neighborhoods" is telling: not long ago, a mayor had to relocate all the families in a block of apartment buildings to allow them to avoid racketeering and drug trafficking. In France today, we have lawless neighborhoods where the police are afraid to enter.

Certain cities in France, and not just in the south, appear more Arab-Muslim than French. It is difficult for a sociologist to put figures on the number of Muslims in France: in France, it is considered insulting and discriminatory to ask someone about their origin and religion and to account for them according to this criterion. The natural consequence is that problems develop in the dark and end up by blowing up in your face. But Fourquet has found a backdoor way of identifying the number of Muslims in France.[1] He studied the first names given in maternity wards over several decades. He was able to recognize, this time with figures, that the first name Marie, which was given to a very large number of little girls until the second half of the twentieth century, had become almost nonexistent and that the first name Mohammed had become the dominant name for boys. It thus became easy to count Muslims; you do not give your boy the name Mohammed without objective reasons. He concluded that in the France of tomorrow, inhabitants from Arab-Muslim backgrounds (be they French citizens or not) will represent one in five, or perhaps one in four, of the inhabitants.

This assessment would not be unsettling in any way if we managed to integrate these populations like before. But what is unsettling is this: according to a survey by the Montaigne Institute (2015), a third of young Muslims in France prefer Sharia law to French law. Are French culture and French mores not enviable? One sometimes wonders by what strange, psychological mechanism it happens that part of this population prefers patriarchy and the subjugation of girls to our emancipated customs. It is because, as of now, they find this single means of identifying with something, since they feel rejected by France. Girls of Arab-Muslim origin integrate much better than boys, go on to study, and have mixed marriages. Their brothers conveniently end up in prison. For a boy from an Islamic background, Western culture is humiliating: he has to give up the unmerited, biological superiority he can claim over women. As one can see, the problems are immense. And because we no longer come to integrate this population, the result is inevitably multiculturalism — in other words, the development of Muslim customs and habits in society. The problem is that France has always rejected multiculturalism, as being contrary to the republican spirit. Hence, the incessant and impassioned debates about the veil, separate swimming pools, halal meat in cafeterias, and burkinis on beaches. The French feel that their society is crumbling into pieces, whereas its primordial character is republicanism — that is, unity. The subtitle of Jérôme Fourquet's book is *Naissance d'une nation multiple et divisée* [The birth of a multifaceted and divided nation]. There is no doubt that there is here an unvoiced anguish, wondering what we are going to become if we are no longer what we are. This gives rise to the increase of radical right-wing parties, which today account for over a third of the electorate.

We do not have the calling to be a multicultural society. It is not in our customs. Or, if this transformation becomes compulsory, it will require a radical and traumatic adaptation. The republican unity to which we aspire and that seems to be our identity, in the same way as empire is Russia's identity, or as time is the Jews' identity, must indeed be translated into a patriotic attachment. But for decades, it has been fashionable to spit on the flag and to consider talk of a homeland as a "Vichy" thing. The United States manages to federate diverse cultures through pride in being American and saluting a common flag. It is necessary to have a link between differences, without which the whole will crumble.

Concern grows because we do not understand anything about the phenomenon in front of which we find ourselves: the spread and radicalization of a religious belief—in this case, Islam. We believed that religion was forever useless. We think of it as folklore, a childish tale to lull children to sleep. When it re-appears with such force, we have no intellectual means of grasping it—no concept, no intuition, just contempt and insults, which are ineffective here. You have here, as Marcel Gauchet puts it, a "blind spot in the French mind."[2] It is extraordinary to read the commentaries in many French media on the subject of Islam: they understand nothing of the religious phenomenon, which to them resembles an unidentified object.

My belief, in the end, is that we must assume our historical responsibility. We colonized many North African and African countries in the nineteenth century. I do not want to judge our ancestors, whose benchmarks were different from ours. But they left to us French-speaking populations overseas, still linked to France by a memory that we do not have the power to erase. In the 1970s and 1980s, we brought in these workers, who were cheaper than the French, to labor in our worksites. It probably was not a good idea (the Swiss preferred to raise the wages of their own workers, which in the long run was smarter), but again,

I am not judging our ancestors. The result is that we now have here an Arab-Muslim world for which we are responsible, because each country bears the historical responsibility for its past actions, just as one bears the awareness and burden of one's father's actions, good or bad. One does not get rid of oneself, and we do not exist only in the fleeting present. We are charged with this question, without being able to be rid of it, because we are accountable for the past as much as for the future.

14

Belonging to Europe

At the start, during the 1990s, a nascent, institutional Europe nurtured the project of forming itself with respect for nations and intermediate communities. Europe's great creators were Christians, opposed to Marxism and bureaucratic centralism — in short, devoted to individual freedom and the autonomy of intermediary governing bodies. It was, thus, at this point that Jacques Delors's cabinet set out to study the principle of subsidiarity in depth, with a view to applying it to institutional Europe.

The principle of subsidiarity is not at all a technical instrument, but an anthropological principle. It pertains primarily to a belief (it is not proven!) that human individuals have a true need to guide their own actions according to their own decisions, even if this means losing efficiency: their autonomy, within certain limits, is more important than their comfort. It is held that personal autonomy is an integral part of the grandeur of the person. It is held that each and every one of us feels that a person exists more on account of the initiative of his or her actions (alone or in a group) than on account of the gifts or benefits bestowed upon him or her. This assertion may seem obvious to our Western ears, which are accustomed to considering individuals as "persons." But it turns out that the application of this principle is quite difficult: the state would have to agree, for example, to let districts or townships be in charge of the public good—and that is not at all French. Here begins the problem of institutional Europe.

At the start, France's strong influence in the construction of Europe contributed significantly to turning Europe into a centralized political edifice. The French built a structure in their own image—the Germans, had they had more influence at that time, would no doubt have been more inspired by federal models. When Jacques Delors arrived as the head of the European Commission, he knew how important the autonomy of individuals and intermediary governing bodies were for the culture of Europe as a whole. However, he was a French mandarin, convinced about the unparalleled value of the state and all that comes from it. He appeals to the principle of subsidiarity, declining it and referring to it by name. And at the same time, he distorts the meaning of it, turning it, in fact, into a Jacobin principle. This misrepresentation is not very difficult to achieve. The principle of subsidiarity holds that the more powerful player should intervene only as a last resort, when the less powerful player, whose action always comes first, is insufficient. In order to use subsidiarity as a pretext for Jacobinism, all you have to do is declare the inadequacy of all the players. Moreover, this so-called insufficiency, a relative term, is understood in terms of a standard of the common good that naturally depends on time and place. It therefore suffices to decree, when necessary, a very high level of the common good. If, for example, the ecological common good that is required is the ecological level of

Denmark, then all other countries will be declared insufficient and will lose their autonomy to Europe. This is how institutional Europe has imposed its diktats on nations, while claiming to be a follower of the principle of subsidiarity, a principle of autonomy. It has to be said that the nations willingly lent themselves to this evolution. Institutional Europe has, over the years, become a vast, centralized technocracy, governed by a liberal-libertarian current of thought that has replaced Marxism among Europe's elites.

First, there is a centralized technocracy. These words are telling. Europe is governed not by elected representatives but by "commissioners," not by laws but by "directives." The entire vocabulary is indicative of technocracy: government is a science, thus, without debate or critiques; it is just and true by its mere utterance. In his 1999 speech in the Strasbourg Cathedral, Jacques Delors specified Europe as "a structure with a technocratic feel, progressing under the aegis of a type of gentle and enlightened despotism." Technocracy is the realm of abstraction, a domain of ideas. Efficiency and output are sought after, without the asking of other questions. In a technocracy, those who govern are not elected, and the people who are supposed to be responsible are not known and, as a result, are not responsible; authorities are anonymous, and decisions are shrouded by a veil of ignorance. This offends many commentators and intellectuals.[1]

To rely on technocracy is just pragmatism — in other words, using the right means to become wealthy; materialism is the only "philosophy" on which all people can agree, because it assumes no value, other than comfort, that someone can criticize. So it is that the technocracy in Brussels has a liberal economic policy. And since it recognizes no discussion, it imposes this policy on nations. What came about — within certain limits, at any rate — was a windfall for France. Anchored in its socialist nostalgia and Colbertist piety, France was forced to embrace liberalism when it joined Europe. This probably freed it from a few old demons, of which it would have had difficulty ridding itself on its own. Several powerful corporations with shameful privileges, such as Air France, have lost their supremacy and should have had to understand what competition is, for the greater good of their passengers. However, we gauge the inconvenience of having to carry out a reform imposed from the outside, and not one desired from within. For a long time, France was organized like the society described in Fichte's *The Closed Commercial State*, an economy of monopolies whose aim was not the well-being of consumers, but that of employees and the security of their jobs. The French, still steeped in socialist nostalgia, lived through these forced liberal reforms with rebellion and bitterness, which, incidentally, continue today (hence, the Rebellious France party, led by Jean-Luc Mélenchon). Only France would have 20 percent of its people still be *leftists*, people who embody the resentment of orphaned socialists and who are incensed by compulsory liberal reforms. What many French people would prefer, instead of seeing France operate in the liberal way that Europe wants, is to see Europe adopt French methods and, for example, extend our social laws to other countries on the continent.

Technocracy can be built only through the elimination of previous cultural references and the creation of abstractions. The history of each nation is swept under the rug, along with its common culture. In this respect, the deliberate erasure of Europe's Christian roots is significant. At a time when a draft of the European constitution was being drawn up, the question of the affirmation of Christian roots was posed to the European Council. Germany, Italy, Spain, Portugal, the United Kingdom, Greece, and Poland were in favor of such a reference in the constitution. Jacques Chirac was against it, along with Sweden and Belgium. Christian roots would not be mentioned. On the occasion of the fifteen-hundredth anniversary of Cyril and Methodius, when

Slovakia minted the likeness of these saints on the national side of its two-euro coin, France protested and, followed by the European Commission, demanded that the crosses and halos of these saints be removed. Or, when Viktor Orbán had "the unifying virtue of Christianity for the Hungarian nation" included in the preamble to the new Hungarian constitution, the European Parliament questioned such an endorsement during heated debates. Europe is a palace of concepts, which is as abstract as its banknotes, which display only fictitious monuments. It exposes traditions and customs to trial by public opinion. From behind a neutral, technical exterior, it seeks to impose on all its territories the postmodern ideology of the most complete, individualistic emancipation possible. Everything is done to ensure that "latecomer" countries (e.g., Ireland, Poland) also adopt in full force the societal laws, without any debate being possible. Emmanuel Macron and Angela Merkel perfectly reflect the "progressive" ideology desired by Europe: globalism, multiculturalism, individualism, and unlimited emancipation. Their opponents, who are labeled with the insulting adjective of "populist," but who would be more accurately described as "antiliberal," are stricken with indignity, and here you have the entirety of the sickness of today's Europe (and of the West in general). "Progressives," on the European as well as the national levels, do not want opponents with whom they debate; they want only enemies who represent Evil par excellence.

It is this ideological character of institutional Europe that, at the turn of the century, Central European countries viewed with fear, and it is against this that they are erecting alternative governments. "Populist" movements are attempts to find again instances of rootedness that have been erased by common institutions: rootedness in traditional religion, in the family, and in cultural identity. They attempt to resist the prevailing libertarianism and multiculturalism.

It is consistent with institutional Europe, and also is healthy, to have opposing points of view on whether to legitimize marriage between two people of the same sex, or how to welcome refugees, and in what number. On the other hand, what is neither healthy nor consistent is for one of these two currents to arrogate right and legitimacy to itself alone, leaving the other current in disgrace: this is THE problem with Europe today. France, along with Germany, is the country that is trying to lead the others in this direction.

Conclusion

The notion of *relegation* seems to me to be the most apt way to characterize the misfortune of France in the twenty-first century. There are many countries that, convinced that they are greater than others, find themselves humiliated because they have been lowered to the common measuring stick—and this humiliation produces disasters—for example, in Germany in the middle of the twentieth century or in Russia today. But France, on the other hand, considers itself to be bestowed with social and cultural greatness: a superior language, an incomparable way of life, and a "social model" without rival. The French are troubled to see their model being erased, with, moreover, the complicity of their elite.[1] Whereas they have always been convinced that they were capable of showing others the correct path to social equality, today they can see themselves obliged to adopt the more liberal and competitive models of the outside world.

If one tries to examine the collapse of this social model as objectively as possible, then it is necessary to look at other European welfare states. In the Scandinavian countries, social redistribution is just as important as in France, and yet these systems function without overburdening the future. That is because in these countries, the way that the redistribution is managed is quite different: the system is rendered sustainable by requiring users and citizens to be responsible. It could be argued that what is exhausting France (exhausted hospitals, an exhausted national educational system) is not the nature of the system itself, but that the system permits its participants and clients to be irresponsible. The system of redistribution (e.g., the green card for health care) is not disastrous in itself; it becomes disastrous when one turns a blind eye to the millions of abuses of the said card. In other words, it is less necessary to blame the model itself than the weakness and cowardice of those who govern when applying the model with the rigor that it, in itself, demands. For the more generous an organization is, the more it must be on guard that this generosity not be abused. And France's leaders, whether on the left or the right, are absolutely not capable of that necessary rigor. So, not only does the welfare system facilitate natural vices like cheating and laziness; it aids in their development. Always complaining and never blaming, demanding nothing but conceding everything, the French welfare system produces a population of spoiled children, always pampered but never content. It could be said that a social model that is so generous, but so corrupted by general laxity, was able to function during a period of great wealth, the Thirty Glorious Years, but that today it can no longer do so, as it would need the Danaids' barrel in order to survive.

Yet when confronted with this fallen paragon, the French do not understand, and they consider themselves victims of a twist of fate. What? In order to survive, it would be necessary for them to become like everyone else — that is, to live in an "ultraliberal" society where Uber-ization is the rule and where schools and hospitals are not free, as in the United States, the land of the Wild West, where survival of the fittest prevails. This is why France is depressed: when asked when they would have liked to have lived, 70 percent of French people responded "in the past," and only 5 percent said "in the future."[2]

It is probably necessary to add one last clarification. Since the revolution of 1789, France has been submerged in ideology, first Jacobin, then socialist, and then Marxist. It has literally been permeated with the expectation of *a brighter future*. This lost hope gives way to a great, bemused emptiness — but for all of this, a lack of realism has not disappeared. Hervé Le Bras and Emmanuel Todd have shown that in French regions that were formerly de-Christianized and that then became communist, the fall of communism provoked "a moral collapse"[3] — formerly Catholic regions fared better in terms of integrating individuals.

How can the world's most redistributive country, and one of its wealthiest, also happen to be one of the most unhappy? French unhappiness stems from our ideological passion. The paradox between prosperity (real, quantifiable) and pessimism (obvious, describable) stems from the deeply ideological nature of its people. France has been conditioned so much by socialism and egalitarianism of every type that the mediocrity of our all-too-human existence seems to be unbearable to us. It is utopia that depresses us. France certainly does not suffer from a lack of finance, talent, or luck: it suffers from being unrealistic.

The dreaded claim that "it was better before" is shared by all the radical parties, which now make up more than half the electorate, right and left. This melancholy and regret about the past, for some, stems from the loss of an overarching ideology: Marxism and all its fallen dreams. For others, it is the rejection of the present state of the world, and in particular the waves of immigration. A minimum of pragmatism would require us to understand that communism's total equality for all does not exist and, moreover, that waves of immigration, and undoubtedly multiculturalism, are now a part of life. (We could avoid multiculturalism and integrate the immigrants who are here, but only if we set up a completely decentralized Swiss-style system, which we do not want at any cost: our Jacobinism takes precedence over our desire for integration.) It is as chimerical to want to return to the past as it is to create utopias, and in this respect, we can juxtapose the reactionary spirit of Zemmour–Le Pen and the utopian spirit of Mélenchon. For utopia will never exist, and as for the past, one can love it if one wants and cherish photos of it, but in any case, one can never go back there.

We are dramatically lacking in pragmatism: a country of dreamers who fall into melancholy when reality catches up with them; a country with immense resources, whose spirit is such that it is constantly inventing, but one that is so ignorant of common sense and, in the end, so infantile. As I finish this manuscript, Emmanuel Macron has just been elected president of the republic for the second time: a Pyrrhic victory, since it was achieved at the cost of altering the democratic spirit. The classic right and left, which have alternately governed the country for decades, together account for 6 percent of the vote. . . . The president, having received barely one-third of the vote, finds himself alone in a climate with 60 percent of protest votes, those on the far left or far right, people who are seen as, in the words of Hillary Clinton, a "basket of deplorables" and excluded from the famous "circle of reason"—in other words, people literally pushed into the streets. This denial of democracy, coupled with bureaucratic imperialism and abysmal debt, gives rise to serious worries. One cannot look down on more than half the electorate with impunity. In this respect, France expresses a situation common in the contemporary West, starting with the United States: the violent, bellicose, furious partition of the elites and the people, which, instead of being expressed in democratic debate, escalates into a murderous denigration of the latter by the former. All the while, our young president is caressing the immortal French temptation: that of Bonapartism. Centuries pass, but the spirit remains. We have a long way to go before we reach democratic maturity.

NOTES

Introduction : French Malaise

1. Translator's Note: "Les Trente Glorieuses," or "The Glorious Thirty Years," is the period of economic and cultural growth, prosperity, and change in France between 1945 and 1975.

2. Olivennes, *Le délicieux malheur français*, 11, 34.

3. Giraudoux, *Souvenir de deux existences*, 85.

CHAPTER 1. Identity, History

1. Cicero, *De re publica; De legibus*, 211–13.

2. Gauchet, *Comprendre le malheur français*, 39ff.

3. Translator's note: Emil Cioran (1911–95) was a Romanian philosopher.

4. Bernanos, *La vocation spirituelle de la France.*

5. Keyserling, *Europe.*

6. A country spoiled not only by its variety and its propitious nature, but also by the history that spares it of destructions—our two thousand Romanesque churches still stand. Louis-Fernand Céline, in the first pages of *Voyage au bout de la nuit*, translates this thought

into his splendid and mischievous language: "What you call a race is nothing but a collection of riffraff like me, bleary-eyed, flea-bitten, chilled to the bone. They came here from the four corners of the earth, driven by hunger, plague, tumors and the cold, and stopped here. They couldn't go any further because of the ocean. That's France, that's the French people." Céline, *Journey to the End of the Night*, 3–4.

CHAPTER 2.   Republic vs. Democracy

1. Girardet, *Mythes et mythologies politiques*.
2. Aristotle, *Politics* 2.5.1263a25–30 (McKeon, 1151). [Translator's note: In the text, I have translated the author's quotation from a French translation of Aristotle's *Politics*. The English translation of this passage from McKeon reads: "Property should be in a certain sense in common, but as a general rule, private; for, when every one has a distinct interest, men will not complain of one another, and they will make more progress, because every one will be attending to his own business. And yet, by reason of goodness, and in respect of use, 'Friends,' as the proverb says, 'will have all things in common.'"]
3. Fourquet, *L'archipel français*.
4. Furet and Ozouf, *Le siècle de l'avènement républicain*, 46.
5. Kriegel, *Philosophie de la république*, 1–20.

CHAPTER 3.   Jacobinism and Bonapartism

1. Herodotus, *Histories* 5.92.2.
2. Translator's note: The author alludes to Charles Maurras (1868–1952), a French writer and political theorist.
3. Tocqueville, *Old Regime and the Revolution*, 125.
4. Tocqueville, *Old Regime and the Revolution*, 125.
5. Zeldin, *Histoire des passions françaises*, 2:484.
6. Grenouilleau, *Nos petites patries*.

CHAPTER 4. A Distant and Maternal Government

1. Voltaire, "Letter CCCVIII to d'Alembert."
2. Proudhon, *Théorie de l'impôt*.
3. Bertauld, *Philosophie politique de la France*.
4. Gouguenheim, *La réforme grégorienne*.

CHAPTER 5. Status and Positions

1. D'Iribarne, *L'étrangeté française*, 218.
2. Tocqueville, *Old Regime and the Revolution*, 1:231.
3. Keyserling, *Europe*, 48.
4. D'Iribarne, *L'étrangeté française*.
5. Gauchet, *Comprendre le malheur français*, 224.
6. Gauchet, *Comprendre le malheur français*, 435. [Translator's note: The night of August 4th, 1789, was when the French National Assembly abolished the feudal system and its attendant rights in France.]

CHAPTER 6. The Anthropology of Defiance:
Envy, Equality, and Mistrust

1. Tocqueville, *Old Regime and the Revolution*, 102.
2. Tocqueville, *Old Regime and the Revolution*, 243.
3. D'Iribarne, *La logique de l'honneur*.
4. Montesquieu, *Spirit of the Laws*, sections 3 and 4.
5. Montesquieu, *Spirit of the Laws*, sections 3 and 4.
6. Le Bras and Todd, *Le mystère français*, 40.
7. Olivennes, *Le délicieux malheur français*, 99.
8. D'Iribarne, *L'étrangeté française*.
9. Olivennes, *Le délicieux malheur français*, 149.
10. Algan and Cahuc, *La société de defiance: Comment le modèle français s'autodétruit*.

11. De Gaulle, *Mémoires d'espoir.*
12. Esping-Andersen, *Les trois mondes de l'État-providence.*

CHAPTER 7. Paris and the Provinces

1. Tocqueville, *Old Regime and the Revolution,* 145–46.
2. Cicero, *De re publica* 1.19.
3. Tocqueville, *Old Regime and the Revolution,* 146–47.
4. Tocqueville, *Old Regime and the Revolution,* 242.
5. Tocqueville, *Old Regime and the Revolution,* 147.
6. Mauriac, *La province,* 19.
7. Heine, *De l'Allemagne,* 42.

CHAPTER 8. Intellectuals

1. Zeldin, *Histoire des passions française,* vol. 2.
2. Tocqueville, *Old Regime and the Revolution,* 148.
3. Tocqueville, *Old Regime and the Revolution,* 210.
4. Sartre, *Critique de la raison dialiectique,* and *Situations IV,* 248-49.
5. Aron, *Opium of the Intellectuals,* 265–94.
6. Tocqueville, *Old Regime and the Revolution,* 246.
7. Gusdorf, *Les revolutions de France et d'Amérique,* 204.

CHAPTER 9. The Right and the Left

1. Patočka, quoted in "Preface from Paul Ricoeur," xii.
2. Moulin, *La gauche, la droite et le péché original.*
3. Trotsky, *Literature and Revolution,* 56–105.
4. Sirinelli, *Histoire des droits en France.*

CHAPTER 10. The People and the Elite

1. Bloch, *L'étrange défaite*, 56.

CHAPTER 11. French Secularism

1. Tocqueville, *Old Regime and the Revolution*, 204–5.
2. Proudhon, *De la justice et de la revolution dans l'église*, 258.

CHAPTER 12. The Present State of Religion

1. Le Bras and Todd, *Le mystère français*, 265.

CHAPTER 13. The Sense of Identity and Immigration

1. Fourquet, *L'archipel français*.
2. Gauchet, *Comprendre le malheur français*, 299, 315.

CHAPTER 14. Belonging to Europe

1. Gauchet, *Comprendre le malheur français*, 196–97.

Conclusion

1. Frank, *La hantise du déclin*.
2. Olivennes, *Le délicieux malheur français*, 76.
3. Le Bras and Todd, *Le mystère français*, 199.

BIBLIOGRAPHY

Algan, Yann, and Pierre Cahuc. *La société de defiance: Comment le modèle français s'autodétruit*. Paris: Éditions de la rue de l'Ulm, 2016.

Aristotle. *Politics*. In *The Basic Works of Aristotle*, translated by Richard McKeon, 1127–1325. New York: Random House, 1941.

Aron, Raymond. *The Opium of the Intellectuals*. Translated by Harvey C. Mansfield. New Brunswick, NJ: Transaction Publishers, 2001.

Baverez, Nicolas. *La France qui tombe*. Paris: Tempus Perrin, 2004.

Bernanos, Georges. *La vocation spirituelle de la France*. Paris: Éditions Plon, 1975.

Bertauld, Alfred. *Philosophie politique de la France*. Paris: Didier et Co, 1861.

Bloch, Marc. *L'étrange défaite*. Paris: Gallimard, 1990.

Céline, Louis-Ferdinand. *Journey to the End of the Night*. Translated by Ralph Manheim. New York: New Directions Books, 1983. Originally published as *Voyage au bout de la nuit* (Paris: Editions Denoël et Steele, 1932).

Cicero, Marcus Tullius. *De re publica; De legibus*. Translated by Clinton Walker Keyes. Cambridge, MA: Harvard University Press, 1959.

de Gaulle, Charles. *Mémoires d'espoir*. Paris: Éditions Plon, 1970.

d'Iribarne, Philippe. *La logique de l'honneur*. Paris: Éditions du Seuil, 1989.

———. *L'étrangeté française*. Paris: Éditions du Seuil, 2006.

Esping-Andersen, G. *Les trois mondes de l'État-providence*. Paris: Presses universitaires de France, 1990.

Fichte, Johann Gottlieb. *The Closed Commercial State*. Translated by Anthony Curtis Adler. Albany: State University of New York Press, 2012.

Fourquet, Jérôme. *L'Archipel français: Naissance d'une nation multiple et divisée*. Paris: Éditions du Seuil, 2019.

Frank, Robert. *La hantise du déclin: La France de 1914 à 2014*. Paris: Belin, 2014.

Furet, François, and Mona Ozouf. *Le siècle de l'avènement républicain*. Paris: Éditions Gallimard, 1993.

Gauchet, Marcel. *Comprendre le malheur français*. Paris: Éditions Stock, 2016.

Girardet, Raoul. *Mythes et mythologies politiques*. Paris: Éditions du Seuil, 1990.

Giraudoux, Jean. *Souvenir de deux existences*. Paris: Grasset, 1975.

Goodhart, David. *The Road to Somewhere: The Populist Revolt and the Future of Politics*. Oxford: Oxford University Press, 2017.

Gouguenheim, Sylvain. *La réforme grégorienne*. Paris: Temps Présent, 2014.

Grenouilleau, Olivier. *Nos petites patries*. Paris: Éditions Gallimard, 2019.

Gusdorf, Georges. *Les revolutions de France et d'Amérique*. Paris: La Table Ronde, 2005.

Heine, Heinrich. *De l'Allemagne*. Paris: Gallimard, 1998.

Herodotus. *The Histories*. Edited by John Marincola. Translated by Aubrey de Sélincourt. New York: Penguin, 2003.

Keyserling, Hermann. *Europe*. Translated by Maurice Samuel. New York: Harcourt Brace, 1928.

Kriegel, Blandine. *Philosophie de la république*. Paris: Plon, 1998.

Le Bras, Hervé. *Se sentir mal dans une France qui va bien: La société paradoxale*. Paris: L'Aube, 2019.

Le Bras, Hervé, and Emmanuel Todd. *Le mystère français*. Paris: Éditions du Seuil, 2013.

Manzoni, Alessandro. *Les fiancés*. Paris: Hachette, 2018.

Mauriac, François. *La province*. Paris: Arléa, 1988.

Montesquieu, Charles de. *The Spirit of the Laws*. Edited and translated by Anne M. Cohler, Basia Carolyn Miller, and Harold Samuel Stone. Cambridge: Cambridge University Press, 1989.

Moulin, Léo. *La gauche, la droite et le péché original.* Paris: Klinksieck, 1984.

Olivennes, Denis. *Le délicieux malheur français.* Paris: Albin Michel, 2019.

Proudhon, Pierre-Joseph. *De la justice et de la revolution dans l'église.* Vol 2. Brussels/Leipzig: A. Schnée, 1860.

———. *Théorie de l'impôt: Question mise au concours par le Conseil d'état du canton de Vaud en 1860.* Brussels: Office de publicité, 1861.

Ricoeur, Paul. "Preface from Paul Ricoeur." In *Heretical Essays in the Philosophy of History*, by Jan Patočka, translated by Erazim Kohák and edited by James Dodd. vii–xvi. La Salle, IL: Open Court, 1999.

Sartre, Jean-Paul. *Critique de la raison dialiectique.* Paris: Éditions Gallimard, 1960.

———. *Situations IV.* Paris: Gallimard, 1964.

Sirinelli, Jean-François. *Histoire des droits en France.* Paris: Gallimard, 2006.

Solzhenitsyn, Aleksandr. *Révolution et mensonge.* Paris: Fayard, 2018.

Strauch-Bonart, Laetitia. *De la France, ce pays que l'on croyait connaître.* Paris: Perrin, 2022.

Tocqueville, Alexis de. *The Old Regime and the Revolution.* Vol. 1. Edited by François Furet and Françoise Mélonio. Translated by Alan S. Kahan. Chicago: University of Chicago Press, 1998.

Trotsky, Leon. *Literature and Revolution.* Translated by Rose Strunsky. Ann Arbor: University of Michigan Press, 1968.

Vermeren, Pierre. *La France qui déclasse.* Paris: Tallandier, 2022.

Voltaire. "Letter CCCVIII to d'Alembert." In *Oeuvres Complètes de Voltaire*, edited by Georges Avenel, 6:765. Paris: Aux bureaux du Siècle, 1869.

Zeldin, Théodore. *Histoire des passions françaises.* Vol. 2. Paris: Éditions du Seuil, 1994.

Zeniter, Alice. *L'art de perdre.* Paris: Éditions Flammarion, 2017. Translated by Frank Wynne as *The Art of Losing* (New York: Farrar, Straus and Giroux, 2021).

INDEX

CHANTAL DELSOL

is professor of philosophy at the University of
Marne-la-Vallée and an elected member of the Académie
des Sciences Morales et Politiques (Institut de France).
She is the author of numerous books, including
La Fin de la Chrétienté (*The End of Christianity*).

ANDREW KELLEY

is professor of philosophy and chair of the Department
of Philosophy and Religious Studies at Bradley University.
He writes on twentieth-century French philosophy and
has translated books from French and German philosophers.

DANIEL J. MAHONEY

is a senior fellow at the Claremont Institute and
professor emeritus at Assumption University.